Notes to a
Science Fiction
Writer

Notes to a Science

Fiction Writer

Ben Bova

Second Edition, Revised and Expanded

Houghton Mifflin Company Boston

Library of Congress Cataloging in Publication Data

Bova, Benjamin W
Notes to a science fiction writer.

Bibliography: p.
1. Science fiction—Authorship. I. Title.
PN3377.5.S3B6   1981   808.3′876   80-26073
ISBN 0-395-30521-7 (pbk.)

Printed in the United States of America

S 10 9 8 7 6 5 4 3 2

Houghton Mifflin paperback 1981

Three of the stories in this collection, "Fifteen Miles," "Men of Good Will," and "Stars, Won't You Hide Me?" were included in another collection of the author's, *Forward In Time,* published in 1973 by Walker Publishing Company, Inc.

A shortened version of "The Shining Ones" was published in the February 1974 *Boy's Life.* The full version as it appears here has never before been published.

Lines from "Desert Places" by Robert Frost which appear in "Fifteen Miles" are from *The Poetry of Robert Frost* edited by Edward Connery Latham, copyright 1936 by Robert Frost, copyright © 1964 by Leslie Frost Ballantine, copyright © 1969 by Holt, Rinehart and Winston, Inc. Reprinted by permission of Holt, Rinehart and Winston, Publishers.

To George Paravicini

Contents

Notes to a
Science Fiction
Writer

Simple failures of craftsmanship, such as spelling and grammar, can very often ruin the effect of an otherwise salable science fiction story.

"No need to worry, Senators. They're from outer space all right, but they're not too intelligent."

1. Introduction: The Slushpile

This book was written in self-defense.

As an editor of fiction—at *Analog Science Fiction* and *Omni* magazines—every week I received some fifty to a hundred story manuscripts from men and women who had never written a piece of fiction before. The manuscripts stacked up on my desk daily and formed what is known in the publishing business as "the slushpile." Every new writer starts in the slushpile. Most writers never get out of it. They simply get tired of receiving rejection after rejection and eventually quit writing.

Yet one of the few real joys an editor gets is to find a solid, interesting, publishable story in the slushpile. It's a thrill akin to finding gold in a desert wasteland. That writer graduates to the rank of published author and never returns to the slushpile again. But such a pleasure is very rare. Most slushpile writers are deadly dull.

1

Editors do not enjoy rejecting stories. No one likes to send bad news back to an aspiring writer. An editor puts a lot of time and effort into reading manuscripts, because an editor's reputation (as well as salary) depends on the writers that the editor handles. When an editor finds a good new writer, it is a boost to the editor's career, as well as to the writer's.

At both *Analog* and *Omni* I personally read all the incoming manuscripts. There were no first readers, no assistant readers. The editor read everything. It made for some very long days. And nights. Long—and frustrating.

Because in story after story I saw the same basic mistakes being made; the same fundamentals of storytelling being ignored. Stories that began with good ideas, or that had stretches of good writing in them, would fall apart and become unpublishable simply because the writer had overlooked—or never knew—the basic principles of storytelling.

There are good ways and poor ways to build a story, just as there are good ways and poor ways to build a house. If the writer does not use good techniques, the story will collapse, just as when a builder uses poor techniques his building collapses.

Every writer must bring three major factors to each story that he or she writes. They are: ideas, artistry, and craftsmanship. Ideas will be discussed later in this book; suffice to say for now that they are nowhere nearly as difficult to find and develop as most new writers fear. Artistry depends on the individual writer's talent and commitment to writing;

no one can teach artistry to a writer, although many have tried. Artistry depends almost entirely on what's inside the writer—innate talent, heart, guts, and drive. Craftsmanship *can* be taught, and it is the one area where new writers consistently fall short. In most cases, it is simple lack of craftsmanship that prevents a writer from leaving the slushpile. Like a carpenter who has never learned to drive nails straight, writers who have not learned craftsmanship will get nothing but pain for their efforts.

That is why this book was written: to help new writers learn a few things about the craftsmanship that goes into successful stories. This book deals with short-story writing and concentrates on the science fiction short story. There are three main reasons for this:

1. Most new writers cut their teeth on short stories before tackling something bigger and more complex.

2. In today's commercial fiction market, science fiction is one of the few areas open to new short-story writers. Mysteries, gothics, and romances are all much more limited and specialized, especially for the short-story writer; but science fiction is as wide open as the infinite heavens. Science fiction magazines actively seek new writers, and the science fiction community is quick to recognize new talent.

3. Science fiction presents to a writer challenges and problems that cannot be found in other forms of fiction. In addition to all the usual problems of writing, science fiction stories must also have strong and believable scientific or

technical backgrounds. Isaac Asimov has often declared that writing science fiction is more difficult than any other kind of writing. He should know; he's written everything from mysteries to learned tomes on the Bible and Shakespeare. If you can handle science fiction skillfully, chances are you will be able to write other types of fiction or nonfiction with ease.

Science fiction has become known as "the literature of ideas"; so much so that some critics have disparagingly pointed out that many SF stories have The Idea as their hero, with very little else to recommend them. Ideas *are* important in science fiction. They are a necessary ingredient of any good SF tale. But the ideas themselves should not be the be-all and end-all of every story.

Very often it is the idea content of good science fiction that attracts new writers to this exciting yet demanding field. (And please note that *new* writers are not necessarily youngsters; many men and women turn to writing science fiction after establishing successful careers for themselves in other fields.) Science fiction's "sense of wonder" attracts new writers. And why not? Look at the playground they have for themselves! There's the entire universe of stars and galaxies, and all of the past, present, and future to write about. Science fiction stories can be set anywhere and anywhen. There's interstellar flight, time travel, immortality, genetic engineering, biofeedback, behavior control, telepathy and other Extra-Sensory Powers (ESP), colonizing space, developing new technologies, exploring the vast cosmos or the inner landscapes of the mind.

But even more fascinating for the writer (and the reader) of science fiction is the way these ideas can be used to develop stories about *people*. That is what all of fiction is about: people. In science fiction, some of the "people" may look very nonhuman; they may live on strange, wild, exotic worlds. They will always face incredible problems and strive to surmount them. Sometimes they will win, sometimes lose. But they will always *strive,* because at the core of every good science fiction story is the very fundamental faith that we can use our own intelligence to understand the world and solve our problems.

All those weird backgrounds and fantastic ideas, all those special ingredients of science fiction, are really a set of tricks that the writers use to place their characters in the kinds of desperate situations where they will have to do their very best, or their very worst, to survive. For all of fiction is an examination of the human spirit, placing that spirit in a crucible where we can test its true worth. In science fiction we can go far beyond the boundaries of here and now, to put that crucible any place and any time we want to, and make the testing fire as hot as can be imagined.

That is science fiction's special advantage, and its special challenge: going beyond the boundaries of the here-and-now to test the human spirit in new and ever-more-powerful ways.

The plan of this book is straightforward. I assume that you want to write publishable science fiction short stories. I will speak directly to you, just as if we were sitting together in my office discussing craftsmanship face to face.

We will talk about the four main aspects of short-story writing: character, background, conflict, and plot. Four short science fiction stories of mine will serve as models to illustrate the points we discuss. There are myriads of better and more popular stories to use as examples, of course. I am using four of my own because I know *exactly* how and why they came to be written, what problems they presented to the writer, when they were published, where they met my expectations, and where they failed.

Each of the four areas of study—character, background, conflict, and plot—will be divided into two sections: one on theory, the other on practice. To begin, the first chapter will be "Character: Theory." After it, we will have the short story that serves as an example, followed by a chapter on "Character: Practice," showing how the theoretical ideas were handled in the actual story.

Finally, there will be a chapter on the science fiction market and a wrap-up chapter in which we discuss ideas, the mechanical aspects of manuscript preparation, and a few other things.

Now a few words on what this book is *not*.

It is not an exhaustive textbook on the techniques of writing. I assume that you know how to construct an English sentence and how to put sentences together into readable paragraphs. We will not spend a chapter, or even a few pages, discussing what a viewpoint character is, or how to handle flashbacks, or the proper use of adjectives and adverbs. All these things you should have acquired in high school English classes. If you don't understand them now, go back and learn them before going any further.

There are many graduates of high school, and even college courses in creative writing, who have been taught how to write lovely paragraphs, but who have never learned how to construct a *story*. Creative writing courses hardly ever teach story construction. This book deals with construction techniques. It is intended as a practical guide for those who want to write commercial fiction and sell it to magazine and book editors.

We will concentrate on the *craft* of writing, on the techniques of telling a story in print. Some critics consider this too simple, too mechanistic, for aspiring writers to care about. But, as I said earlier, it is the poor craftsmanship of most stories that prevents them from being published.

Good story-writing certainly has a mechanical side to it. You can't get readers interested in a boring, idiotic hero any more than you can get someone to buy a house that has no roof.

Since the time when storytelling began, probably back in the Ice Age, people have developed workable, usable, successful techniques for telling their tales. Storytellers use those techniques today, whether they are sitting around a campfire or in a Hollywood office. The techniques have changed very little over the centuries because the human brain has not changed. We still receive information and assimilate it in our minds in the same way our ancestors did. Our basic neural wiring has not changed, so the techniques of storytelling, of putting information into that human neural wiring, are basically unchanged.

Homer used these techniques. So did Goethe and Shakespeare.

And so will you, if and when you become a successful storyteller. I hope this book will help you along that path.

2. Character: Theory

All fiction is based on character.

That is, every fiction story hinges on the writer's handling of the people in the story. In particular, it is the central character, or *protagonist*, who makes the difference between a good story and a bad one.

In fact, you can define a short story as: the prose description of a character attempting to solve a problem— nothing more. And nothing less.

In science fiction, the character need not be a human being. Science fiction stories have been written in which the protagonist was a robot, an alien from another world, a supernatural being, an animal, or even a plant. But in each case, the story was successful only if the protagonist—no matter what he/she/it looked like or was made of— *behaved like a human being.*

Readers come to stories for enjoyment. They don't want to be bored or confused. They don't want to be preached at. If a reader starts a story about a machine, or a tree, or a pintail duck, and the protagonist has no human traits at all—it simply grinds its gears, or sways in the wind, or lays eggs—the reader will quickly put the story down and turn to something else. But give the protagonist a human problem, such as survival, and let it struggle to solve that problem, and the reader will be able to enjoy the story.

A story is like any other form of entertainment. It must catch the audience's interest, and then hold it. A story has enormous advantages over every other form of entertainment, because the written word can appeal directly to the reader's imagination. A writer can unlock the reader's imagination and take him on an exciting journey to strange and wonderful lands, using nothing more than ink and paper. A writer doesn't need a crew of actors, directors, musicians, stagehands, cameramen, or props, sets, curtains, lights. All a writer needs is a writing tool, with which to speak *directly* to the reader.

On the other hand, the writer never meets the reader. You can't stand at a reader's elbow and explain the things that puzzle him; you can't advise the reader to skip the next few paragraphs because they're really not necessary to his understanding of the story, and should have been taken out. The writer must put down everything he wants to say, in print, and hope that the reader will see and hear and feel and taste and smell all the things that the writer wants to get across in the story. You're asking the reader to understand what was in your mind while you were writing, to understand it by deciphering those strange ink marks on the paper.

Your job, as a writer, is to make the reader *live in* your story. You must make the reader forget that he's sitting in a rather uncomfortable chair, squinting at the page in poor light, while all sorts of distractions poke at him. You want that reader to believe that he is actually in the world of your imagination, the world you have created, climbing up that mountain you've written about, struggling against the cold and ice to find the treasure that you planted up at the peak.

The easiest way—in fact the *only* good way—to make the reader live in your story is to give him a character that he wants to be.

Let the reader imagine that he is David Hawkins, being chased by pirates across Treasure Island. Let the reader live the life of Nick Adams, or Tugboat Annie or Sherlock Holmes or Cinderella.

How do you do this? There are two major things to keep in mind.

First, remember that a short story is essentially the description of a character struggling to solve a problem. Pick your central character with care. The protagonist must be interesting enough, and have a grave enough problem, to make the reader care about him or her. Often the protagonist is called the *viewpoint character,* because the story is told from that character's point of view. It is the protagonist's story that you are telling, and he or she must be strong enough to carry the story.

Select a protagonist (or viewpoint character) who has great strengths and at least one glaring weakness, and then give him a staggering problem. Think of Hamlet, Shakespeare's Prince of Denmark. He was strong, intelligent, handsome, loyal, a natural leader; yet he was indecisive, uncertain of himself, and this was his eventual undoing. If Hamlet had been asked to lead an army, or woo a lady, or get straight A's at the university, he could have done it easily. But Shakespeare gave him a problem that preyed on his weakness, not his strength. This is what every good writer must do. Once you've decided who your protagonist will be, and you know his strengths and weaknesses, hit him where it hurts most! Develop an instinct for the jugular. Give your main character a problem that he cannot solve, and then make it as difficult as possible for him to wriggle out of his dilemma.

And don't let him know that he'll win. Many stories are written in which a very capable and interesting protagonist faces a monumental set of problems. Then he goes about solving them without ever trembling, doubting himself, or even perspiring! The protagonist knows he's safe and will be successful, because the writer knows how the story's going to end. This makes for an unbelievable and boring story. Who's going to worry about the world cracking in half, when the hero doesn't worry about it? Certainly not the reader!

The reader must be hanging on tenterhooks of doubt and suspense up until the very end of the story. Which means that the protagonist must be equally in doubt about the outcome. And in a well-crafted story the protagonist *cannot win* unless he surrenders something of inestimable value to himself. In other words, he's got to lose something, and the reader will be in a fever of anticipation trying to figure out what he's going to lose.

The unruffled, supercool, capable hero is one of the

most widespread *stereotypes* of science fiction. Like all stereotypes, he makes for a boring and unbelievable story.

When a writer stocks his story with stereotypes—the brilliant but eccentric physicist, the beautiful but brainless blond secretary, the blue-jeaned antiestablishment hero, the cackling dope-pushing villain—he's merely signalling to the editor that he hasn't thought very deeply about his story.

Stereotype characters are prefabricated parts. Somebody else created these types, long ago, and the new writer is merely borrowing them. They are old, shopworn, and generally made of cardboard. A good writer is like a good architect: every story you create should be an original, with characters and settings designed specifically for that individual story. Not somebody else's prefabricated parts.

Writers who go into the prefab business are called "hacks," and a new writer who *starts* as a hack never gets very far. It's bad enough to turn into a hack once you've become established—and many of the most famous writers on the best seller lists have done that. So have some science fiction writers, alas.

Look around you. You are surrounded by characters every day. How many stereotypes do you see? A jovial Irishman? A singing Italian? A chalk-dusty schoolteacher? An arrogant policeman? An officious administrator?

Look a little deeper. If you begin to study these people, and get to know them, you'll find that every one of them is an individual. Each has a unique personality, a distinct set of problems, habits, joys, and fears. These are the characters you should write about. Watch them carefully. Study their strengths and weaknesses. Stress the points that make them different from everyone else, the traits that are uniquely theirs.

Ask yourself what kinds of problems would hurt them the worst. Then get to your typewriter and tell the world about it.

The second major point about characterization is to show the entire story through the protagonist's point of view.

Even if you write the story in the third person, put nothing on paper that the protagonist has not experienced first hand. This limits you, I know. The protagonist must be in every scene, and you can't tell the reader anything that the protagonist doesn't know. But in return for these problems you get a story that is immediate and real. When the protagonist is puzzled, the reader is puzzled; when the protagonist feels pain, the reader aches; when the protagonist wins against all odds, the reader triumphs. In other words, the reader has been *living* the story. Not merely reading some words off a page.

You might be tempted to write the story in the first person:

I felt the wind whipping at my clothes, cold and sharp and stinging. My pulse was roaring in my ears. I looked down; it was a long way to fall . . .

But you can get almost the same sense of immediacy from a third-person viewpoint, if you restrict yourself to writing only what the protagonist senses:

He felt the wind whipping at his clothes, cold and sharp and stinging. His pulse was roaring in his ears. He looked down; it was a long way to fall . . .

This kind of close and immediate third-person viewpoint has the benefit of being far enough removed from the protagonist so that you can be a little more objective about him. For example, it's very tough to make your protagonist describe himself:

I'm six-feet tall and very solidly built. My hair is blond and wavy; girls like to run their fingers through it.

In the third-person viewpoint, the same description doesn't sound obnoxious at all:

Jack was six-feet tall and very solidly built. His hair was blond and wavy; girls liked to run their fingers through it.

Also, when you write in the third person, you can step away from the protagonist if it's absolutely necessary to tell the reader something that the protagonist doesn't know:

Despite Jack's good looks, Sheryl hated him. She had never let him know this; she wanted him to think . . .

This kind of information sometimes has to be given to the reader. But think long and hard before you step away from your viewpoint character. It can be a very dangerous step, more confusing to the reader than helpful. The best rule is to stay with the protagonist at all times, unless it is absolutely impossible to say what needs to be said.

The well-known SF writer Poul Anderson uses his protagonist's five senses to make certain that the story has as much sensory reality as possible. He checks each page of the story to see how many of the protagonist's senses are used. If a page has nothing but what the protagonist saw, or only what he heard, Anderson rewrites that page so that the sense of touch, or taste, or smell, comes into play. It's astounding how much more vivid that makes a story.

Where do you find a strong protagonist, and what kind of problems can you give him?

Every story you write will be at least partially autobiographical, and every protagonist you create will have more than a little of yourself in him. That's what makes writing such an emotional pursuit; you are revealing yourself, putting your heart and guts out on public display, every time you write a story. When a story is rejected, or a published story is battered by the critics, or fails to sell well—it's as if you are being kicked, folded, stapled, and mutilated. When a story sells, or someone tells you he liked it, or it wins an award—there is no amount of money in the world that can buy that feeling of elation. Each story you write is a part of you. Writers don't use ink, they use their own blood. And the reason most people stop writing is because they can't stand the emotional strain, or they don't have the emotional *need* to write.

All this adds up to a simple fact: Your protagonists will be *you*, to a large degree, together with some mixture from people you know. Beginning writers are always advised to write about people and things that they know first hand. Experienced writers are never told this, because they have learned the lesson thoroughly. No one ever writes about anything that he hasn't experienced first hand. Never. It can't be done.

Really? In a few moments you are going to read "Fifteen Miles," a story about a man trying to walk across fifteen miles of the moon's surface; an astronaut who is dragging back the injured body of a fellow astronaut. I haven't been to the moon. I've never had to carry an injured friend through a wilderness for fifteen feet, let alone fifteen miles. So where's my first-hand experience?

I know the people in that story first hand. I have lived with Chester Arthur Kinsman in my head for a quarter-century. I've written dozens of short stories and several novels about him; almost all of them were rejected, and even "Fifteen Miles" was bounced by the first editor I sent it to. Kinsman and I learned to write together. Father Lemoyne and Bok, the astronomer, are also people I know—composites of many people whom I've met and worked with over the past couple of decades.

"Fifteen Miles" was written before the Apollo program put astronauts on the moon. But it could not have been written before space probes such as *Ranger* and *Surveyor* photographed the lunar surface so thoroughly. I wrote the story literally surrounded by photos and maps of the area in which the action takes place. I worked in the aerospace industry for many years, and became as familiar as I could with the kinds of equipment that will be used when we return to the moon for explorations longer than the Apollo astronauts' brief visits. I have met and worked with the people involved in the space program. I have watched and read volumes of testimony before congressional committees, which is where the quotation that opens the story comes from.

All this is first-hand experience, of a kind. To this experience must come a touch of imagination. That touch came to me when I read Jack London's story "To Light a Fire." As I *lived* London's story and felt the bitter cold of the Yukon freezing me, somewhere deep in the back of my mind a tiny voice said to me, "If Jack London were alive today, he'd still be writing stories about men struggling against the wilderness . . . but they'd be set on the moon, rather than on earth."

Immediately the title, "Fifteen Miles," formed itself in my mind. I wanted to do a story about how difficult it might be to walk across fifteen miles of lunar landscape.

But that was just the bare idea. There was no story in my head. Not until good old Chet Kinsman popped up and said, "Hey, this is my story. Remember where you left me the last time, in 'Test in Orbit'? Well, this 'Fifteen Miles' is the sequel to that story."

He was right. I gave Kinsman the task of making that fifteen-mile walk, and burdened him with a set of problems to make the situation as difficult as possible. I nearly killed him.

Which is what good story-writing is all about.

3. FIFTEEN MILES

"Any word from him yet?"

"Huh? No, nothing."

Kinsman swore to himself as he stood on the open platform of the little lunar rocket jumper.

"Say, where are you now?" The astronomer's voice sounded gritty with static in Kinsman's helmet earphones.

"Up on the rim. He must've gone inside the damned crater."

"The rim? How'd you get . . ."

"Found a flat spot for the jumper. Don't think I walked this far, do you? I'm not as nutty as the priest."

"But you're supposed to stay down here on the plain! The crater's off-limits."

"Tell it to our holy friar. He's the one who marched up

here. I'm just following the seismic rigs he's been planting every three–four miles.''

He could sense Bok shaking his head. "Kinsman, if there're twenty officially approved ways to do a job, you'll pick the twenty-second.''

"If the first twenty-one are lousy.''

"You're not going inside the crater, are you? It's too risky.''

Kinsman almost laughed. "You think sitting in that aluminum casket of yours is *safe?*''

The earphones went silent. With a scowl, Kinsman wished for the tenth time in an hour that he could scratch his twelve-day beard. *Get zipped into the suit and the itches start.* He didn't need a mirror to know that his face was haggard, sleepless, and his black beard was mean looking.

He stepped down from the jumper—a rocket motor with a railed platform and some equipment on it, nothing more—and planted his boots on the solid rock of the ringwall's crest. With a twist of his shoulders to settle the weight of the pressure suit's bulky backpack, he shambled over to the packet of seismic instruments and fluorescent marker that the priest had left there.

"He came right up to the top, and now he's off on the yellow brick road, playing moon explorer. Stupid bastard.''

Reluctantly, he looked into the crater Alphonsus. The brutally short horizon cut across its middle, but the central peak stuck its worn head up among the solemn stars. Beyond it was nothing but dizzying blackness, an abrupt end to the solid world and the beginning of infinity.

Damn the priest! God's gift to geology . . . and I've got to play guardian angel for him.

"Any sign of him?"

Kinsman turned back and looked outward from the crater. He could see the lighted radio mast and squat return rocket, far below on the plain. He even convinced himself that he saw the mound of rubble marking their buried base shelter, where Bok lay curled safely in his bunk. It was two days before sunrise, but the Earthlight lit the plain well enough.

"Sure," Kinsman answered. "He left me a big map with an X to mark the treasure."

"Don't get sore at me!"

"Why not? You're sitting inside. I've got to find our fearless geologist."

"Regulations say one man's got to be in the base at all times."

But not the same one man, Kinsman flashed silently.

"Anyway," Bok went on, "he's got a few hours' oxygen left. Let him putter around inside the crater for a while. He'll come back."

"Not before his air runs out. Besides, he's officially missing. Missed two check-in calls. I'm supposed to scout his last known position. Another of those sweet regs."

Silence again. Bok didn't like being alone in the base, Kinsman knew.

"Why don't you come on back," the astronomer's voice returned, "until he calls in. Then you can get him with the jumper. You'll be running out of air yourself before you can find him inside the crater."

"I'm supposed to try."

"But why? You sure don't think much of him. You've been tripping all over yourself trying to stay clear of him when he's inside the base."

Kinsman suddenly shuddered. *So it shows! If you're not careful you'll tip them both off.*

Aloud he said, "I'm going to look around. Give me an hour. Better call Earthside and tell them what's going on. Stay in the shelter until I come back." *Or until the relief crew shows up.*

"You're wasting your time. And taking an unnecessary chance."

"Wish me luck," Kinsman answered.

"Good luck. I'll sit tight here."

Despite himself, Kinsman grinned. Shutting off the radio, he said to himself, "I know damned well you'll sit tight. Two scientific adventurers. One goes over the hill and the other stays in his bunk two weeks straight."

He gazed out at the bleak landscape, surrounded by starry emptiness. Something caught at his memory:

"They can't scare me with their empty spaces," he muttered. There was more to the verse but he couldn't recall it.

"Can't scare me," he repeated softly, shuffling to the inner rim. He walked very carefully and tried, from inside the cumbersome helmet, to see exactly where he was placing his feet.

The barren slopes fell away in gently terraced steps until, more than half a mile below, they melted into the crater floor. *Looks easy . . . too easy.* With a shrug that was weighted down by the pressure suit, Kinsman started to descend into the crater.

He picked his way across the gravelly terraces and crawled feet first down the breaks between them. The bare rocks were slippery and sometimes sharp. Kinsman went slowly, step by step, trying to make certain he didn't puncture the aluminized fabric of his suit.

His world was cut off now and circled by the dark rocks. The only sounds he knew were the creakings of the suit's joints, the electrical hum of its motor, the faint whir of the helmet's air blower, and his own heavy breathing. Alone, all alone. A solitary microcosm. One living creature in the one universe.

> They cannot scare me with their empty spaces
> Between stars—on stars where no human race is.

There was still more to it: the tag line that he couldn't remember.

Finally he had to stop. The suit was heating up too much from his exertion. He took a marker beacon and planted it on the broken ground. The moon's soil, churned by meteors and whipped into a frozen froth, had an unfinished look about it, as though somebody had been blacktopping the place but stopped before he could apply the final smoothing touches.

From a pouch on his belt Kinsman took a small spool of wire. Plugging one end into the radio outlet on his helmet, he held the spool at arm's length and released the catch. He couldn't see it in the dim light, but he felt the spring fire the wire antenna a hundred yards or so upward and out into the crater.

"Father Lemoyne," he called as the antenna drifted in

the moon's easy gravity. "Father Lemoyne, can you hear me? This is Kinsman."

No answer.

Okay. Down another flight.

After two more stops and nearly an hour of sweaty descent, Kinsman got his answer.

"Here . . . I'm here . . ."

"Where?" Kinsman snapped. "Do something. Make a light."

". . . can't . . ." The voice faded out.

Kinsman reeled in the antenna and fired it out again. "Where the hell are you?"

A cough, with pain behind it. "Shouldn't have done it. Disobeyed. And no water, nothing . . ."

Great! Kinsman frowned. *He's either hysterical or delirious. Or both.*

After firing the spool antenna again, Kinsman flicked on the lamp atop his helmet and looked at the radio direction-finder dial on his forearm. The priest had his suit radio open and the carrier beam was coming through even though he was not talking. The gauges alongside the radio-finder reminded Kinsman that he was about halfway down on his oxygen, and more than an hour had elapsed since he had spoken to Bok.

"I'm trying to zero in on you," Kinsman said. "Are you hurt? Can you . . ."

"Don't, don't, don't. I disobeyed and now I've got to pay for it. Don't trap yourself too . . ." The heavy, reproachful voice lapsed into a mumble that Kinsman couldn't understand.

Trapped. Kinsman could picture it. The priest was using a cannister-suit: a one-man walking cabin, a big plex-idomed rigid can with flexible arms and legs sticking out of it. You could live in it for days at a time—but it was too clumsy for climbing. Which is why the crater was off-limits.

He must've fallen and now he's stuck.

"The sin of pride," he heard the priest babbling. "God forgive us our pride. I wanted to find water; the greatest discovery a man can make on the moon. . . . Pride, nothing but pride."

Kinsman walked slowly, shifting his eyes from the direction finder to the roiled, pocked ground underfoot. He jumped across an eight-foot drop between terraces. The finder's needle snapped to zero.

"Your radio still on?"

"No use . . . go back . . ."

The needle stayed fixed. *Either I busted it or I'm right on top of him.*

He turned full circle, scanning the rough ground as far as his light could reach. No sign of the cannister. Kinsman stepped to the terrace edge. Kneeling with deliberate care, so that his backpack wouldn't unbalance and send him sprawling down the tumbled rocks, he peered over.

In a zigzag fissure a few yards below him was the priest, a giant armored insect gleaming white in the glare of the lamp, feebly waving its one free arm.

"Can you get up?" Kinsman saw that all the weight of the cumbersome suit was on the pinned arm. *Banged up his backpack, too.*

The priest was mumbling again. It sounded like Latin.

"Can you get up?" Kinsman repeated.

"Trying to find the secrets of natural creation . . . storming heaven with rockets . . . We say we're seeking knowledge, but we're really after our own glory . . ."

Kinsman frowned. He couldn't see the older man's face, behind the cannister's heavily tinted window.

"I'll have to get the jumper."

The priest rambled on, coughing spasmodically. Kinsman started back across the terrace.

"Pride leads to death," he heard in his earphones. "You know that, Kinsman. It's pride that makes us murderers."

The shock boggled Kinsman's knees. He turned, trembling. "What . . . did you say?"

"It's hidden. The water is here, hidden . . . frozen in fissures. Strike the rock and bring forth water . . . like Moses. Not even God Himself was going to hide this secret from me . . ."

"What did you say," Kinsman whispered, completely cold inside, "about murder?"

"I know you, Kinsman . . . anger and pride. . . . Destroy not my soul with men of blood . . . whose right hands are . . . are . . ."

Kinsman ran away. He fought back toward the crater rim, storming the terraces blindly, scrabbling up the inclines with four-yard-high jumps. Twice he had to turn up the air blower in his helmet to clear the sweaty fog from his faceplate. He didn't dare stop. He raced on, his heart pounding until he could hear nothing else.

But in his mind he still saw those savage few minutes in orbit, when he had been with the Air Force, when he became a killer. He had won a medal for that secret mission; a medal and a conscience that never slept.

Finally he reached the crest. Collapsing on the deck of the jumper, he forced himself to breath normally again, forced himself to sound normal as he called Bok.

The astronomer said guardedly, "It sounds as though he's dying."

"I think his regenerator's shot. His air must be pretty foul by now."

"No sense going back for him, I guess."

Kinsman hesitated. "Maybe I can get the jumper down close to him." *He found out about me.*

"You'll never get him back in time. And you're not supposed to take the jumper near the crater, let alone inside of it. It's too dangerous."

"You want me to just let him die?" *He's hysterical. If he babbles about me where Bok can hear it . . .*

"Listen," the astronomer said, his voice rising, "you can't leave me stuck here with both of you gone! I know the regulations, Kinsman. You're not allowed to risk yourself or the third man on the team to help a man in trouble."

"I know. I know." *But it wouldn't look right for me to start minding regulations now. Even Bok doesn't expect me to.*

"You don't have enough oxygen in your suit to get down there and back again," Bok insisted.

"I can tap some from the jumper's propellant tank."

"But that's crazy! You'll get yourself stranded!"

"Maybe." *It's an Air Force secret. No discharge; just transferred to the space agency. If they find out about it now, I'll be finished. Everybody'll know. No place to hide . . . newspapers, TV, everybody!*

"You're going to kill yourself over that priest. And you'll be killing me too!"

"He's probably dead by now," Kinsman said. "I'll just put a marker beacon there, so another crew can get him when the time comes. I won't be long."

"But the regulations . . ."

"They were written Earthside. The brass never planned on something like this. I've got to go back, just to make sure."

He flew the jumper back down the crater's inner slope, leaning over the platform railing to see his marker beacons as well as listening to their tinny radio beeping. In a few minutes, he was easing the spraddle-legged platform down on the last terrace before the helpless priest.

"Father Lemoyne."

Kinsman stepped off the jumper and made it to the edge of the fissure in four lunar strides. The white shell was inert, the free arm unmoving.

"Father Lemoyne!"

Kinsman held his breath and listened. Nothing . . . wait . . . the faintest, faintest breathing. More like gasping. Quick, shallow, desperate.

"You're dead," Kinsman heard himself mutter. "Give it up, you're finished. Even if I got you out of here, you'd be dead before I could get you back to the base."

The priest's faceplate was opaque to him; he only saw the reflected spot of his own helmet lamp. But his mind filled with the shocked face he once saw in another visor, a face that just realized it was dead.

He looked away, out to the too-close horizon and the uncompromising stars beyond. Then he remembered the rest of it:

> They cannot scare me with their empty spaces
> Between stars—on stars where no human race is.
> I have it in me so much nearer home
> To scare myself with my own desert places.

Like an automaton, Kinsman turned back to the jumper. His mind was blank now. Without thought, without even feeling, he rigged a line from the jumper's tiny winch to the metal lugs in the cannister-suit's chest. Then he took apart the platform railing and wedged three rejoined sections into the fissure above the fallen man, to form a hoisting angle. Looping the line over the projecting arm, he started the winch.

He climbed down into the fissure and set himself as solidly as he could on the bare, scoured smooth rock. Grabbing the priest's armored shoulders, he guided the oversized cannister up from the crevice, while the winch strained silently.

The railing arm gave way when the priest was only partway up, and Kinsman felt the full weight of the monstrous suit crush down on him. He sank to his knees, gritting his teeth to keep from crying out.

Then the winch took up the slack. Grunting, fumbling,

pushing, he scrabbled up the rocky slope with his arms wrapped halfway round the big cannister's middle. He let the winch drag them to the jumper's edge, then reached out and shut off the motor.

With only a hard breath's pause, Kinsman snapped down the suit's supporting legs, so the priest could stay upright even though unconscious. Then he clambered onto the platform and took the oxygen line from the rocket tankage. Kneeling at the bulbous suit's shoulders, he plugged the line into its emergency air tank.

The older man coughed once. That was all.

Kinsman leaned back on his heels. His faceplate was fogging over again. Or was it fatigue blurring his vision?

The regenerator was hopelessly smashed, he saw. *The old bird must've been breathing his own juices.* When the emergency tank registered full, he disconnected the oxygen line and plugged it into a fitting below the regenerator.

"If you're dead, this is probably going to kill me, too," Kinsman said. He purged the entire suit, forcing the contaminating fumes out and replacing them with the oxygen that the jumper's rocket needed to get them back to the base.

He was close enough now to see through the cannister's tinted visor. The priest's face was grizzled, eyes closed. Its usual smile was gone; the mouth hung open limply.

Kinsman hauled him up onto the rail-less platform and strapped him down on the deck. Then he went to the controls and inched the throttle forward just enough to give them the barest minimum of lift.

The jumper almost made it to the crest before its rocket died and bumped them gently on one of the terraces. There was a small emergency tank of oxygen that could have carried them a little farther, Kinsman knew. But he and the priest would need it for breathing.

"Wonder how many Jesuits have been carried home on their shields?" he asked himself as he unbolted the section of decking that the priest was lying on. By threading the winch line through the bolt holes, he made a sort of sled, which he carefully lowered to the ground. Then he took down the emergency oxygen tank and strapped it to the deck-section, too.

Kinsman wrapped the line around his fists and leaned against the burden. Even in the moon's light gravity, it was like trying to haul a truck.

"Down to less than one horsepower," he grunted, straining forward.

For once he was glad that the scoured rocks had been smoothed clean by micrometeors. He would climb a few steps, wedge himself as firmly as he could, and drag the sled up to him. It took a painful half-hour to reach the ringwall crest.

He could see the base again, tiny and remote as a dream. "All downhill from here," he mumbled.

He thought he heard a groan.

"That's it," he said, pushing the sled over the crest, down the gentle outward slope. "That's it. Stay with it. Don't you die on me. Don't put me through this for nothing!"

"Kinsman!" Bok's voice. "Are you all right?"

The sled skidded against a yard-high rock. Scrambling after it, Kinsman answered, "I'm bringing him in. Just shut up and leave us alone. I think he's alive. Now stop wasting my breath."

Pull it free. Push to get it started downhill again. Strain to hold it back . . . don't let it get away from you. Haul it out of craterlets. Watch your step, don't fall.

"Too damned much uphill in this downhill."

Once he sprawled flat and knocked his helmet against the edge of the improvised sled. He must have blacked out for a moment. Weakly, he dragged himself up to the oxygen tank and refilled his suit's supply. Then he checked the priest's suit and topped off his tank.

"Can't do that again," he said to the silent priest. "Don't know if we'll make it. Maybe we can. If neither one of us has sprung a leak. Maybe . . ."

Time slid away from him. The past and future dissolved into an endless now, a forever of pain and struggle, with the heat of his toil welling up in Kinsman drenchingly.

"Why don't you say something?" Kinsman panted at the priest. "You can't die. Understand me? You can't die! I've got to explain it to you . . . I didn't mean to kill her. I didn't even know she was a girl. You can't tell, can't even see a face until you're too close. She must've been just as scared as I was. She tried to kill me. I was inspecting their satellite . . . how'd I know their cosmonaut was a scared kid? I could've pushed her off, didn't have to kill her. But the first thing I knew I was ripping her air lines open. I didn't know she was a girl, not until it was too late. It doesn't make any difference, but I didn't know it, I didn't know . . ."

They reached the foot of the ringwall and Kinsman dropped to his knees. "Couple more miles now . . . straight-away . . . only a couple more . . . miles." His vision was blurred, and something in his head was buzzing angrily.

Staggering to his feet, he lifted the line over his shoulder and slogged ahead. He could just make out the lighted tip of the base's radio mast.

"Leave him, Chet," Bok's voice pleaded from somewhere. "You can't make it unless you leave him!"

"Shut . . . up."

One step after another. Don't think, don't count. Blank your mind. Be a mindless plow horse. Plod along, one step at a time. Steer for the radio mast. . . . Just a few . . . more miles.

"Don't die on me. Don't you . . . die on me. You're my ticket back. Don't die on me, priest . . . don't die . . ."

It all went dark. First in spots, then totally. Kinsman caught a glimpse of the barren landscape tilting weirdly, then the grave stars slid across his view, then darkness.

"I tried," he heard himself say in a far, far distant voice. "I tried."

For a moment or two he felt himself falling, dropping effortlessly into blackness. Then even that sensation died and he felt nothing at all.

A faint vibration buzzed at him. The darkness began to shift, turn gray at the edges. Kinsman opened his eyes and saw the low, curved ceiling of the underground base. The noise was the electrical machinery that lit and warmed and brought good air to the tight little shelter.

"You okay?" Bok leaned over him. His chubby face was frowning worriedly.

Kinsman weakly nodded.

"Father Lemoyne's going to pull through," Bok said, stepping out of the cramped space between the two bunks. The priest was awake but unmoving, his eyes staring blankly upward. His cannister-suit had been removed and one arm was covered with a plastic cast.

Bok explained. "I've been getting instructions from the Earthside medics. They're sending a team up; should be here in another thirty hours. He's in shock, and his arm's broken. Otherwise he seems pretty good . . . exhausted, but no permanent damage."

Kinsman pulled himself up to a sitting position on the bunk and leaned his back against the curving metal wall. His helmet and boots were off, but he was still wearing the rest of his pressure suit.

"You went out and got us," he realized.

Bok nodded. "You were only about a mile away. I could hear you on the radio. Then you stopped talking. I had to go out."

"You saved my life."

"And you saved the priest's."

Kinsman stopped a moment, remembering. "I did a lot of raving out there, didn't I?"

"Well . . . yes."

"Any of it intelligible?"

Bok wormed his shoulders uncomfortably. "Sort of.

It's, uh . . . it's all on the automatic recorder, you know. All conversations. Nothing I can do about it.''

That's it. Now everybody knows.

"You haven't heard the best of it, though," Bok said. He went to the shelf at the end of the priest's bunk and took a little plastic container. "Look at this."

Kinsman took the container. Inside was a tiny fragment of ice, half melted into water.

"It was stuck in the cleats of his boots. It's really water! Tests out okay, and I even snuck a taste of it. It's water all right."

"He found it after all," Kinsman said. "He'll get into the history books now." *And he'll have to watch his pride even more.*

Bok sat on the shelter's only chair. "Chet, about what you were saying out there . . ."

Kinsman expected tension, but instead he felt only numb. "I know. They'll hear the tapes Earthside."

"There've been rumors about an Air Force guy killing a cosmonaut during a military mission, but I never thought . . . I mean . . ."

"The priest figured it out," Kinsman said. "Or at least he guessed it."

"It must've been rough on you," Bok said.

"Not as rough as what happened to her."

"What'll they do about you?"

Kinsman shrugged. "I don't know. It might get out to the press. Probably I'll be grounded. Unstable. It could be nasty."

"I'm . . . sorry." Bok's voice tailed off helplessly.

"It doesn't matter."

Surprised, Kinsman realized that he meant it. He sat straight upright. "It doesn't matter anymore. They can do whatever they want to. I can handle it. Even if they ground me and throw me to the newsmen . . . I think I can take it. I did it, and it's over with, and I can take what I have to take."

Father Lemoyne's free arm moved slightly. "It's all right," he whispered hoarsely. "It's all right."

The priest turned his face toward Kinsman. His gaze moved from the astronaut's eyes to the plastic container, still in Kinsman's hands, and back again. "It's all right," he repeated. "It wasn't hell we were in; it was purgatory. We'll come out all right." He smiled. Then he closed his eyes and his face relaxed into sleep. But the smile remained, strangely gentle in that bearded, haggard face; ready to meet the world or eternity.

4. Character: Practice

"**F**ifteen Miles" dealt with three characters, and each of them had a problem. Chet Kinsman was the viewpoint character, the protagonist. Everything in the story was seen from his point of view. Without him and his problems, there would have been no story.

Notice that Kinsman had problems, plural. That is one major difference between the protagonist of a story and the other characters. Secondary characters can have one fundamental problem to solve. Minor characters needn't have any problems at all. But the protagonist, the person whom the story is all about, the person whom the reader wants to be—the protagonist has a whole complex of problems.

I'm going to borrow a marvelous technique from William Foster-Harris, the fine teacher of writing from the University of Oklahoma. He advises writers to visualize their characters' problems as a simple equation: Emotion A vs. Emotion B. For example, in Kinsman's case, it's *guilt* vs. *duty*. Father Lemoyne is torn by *pride* vs. *obedience*. And Bok's problem is *fear* vs. *responsibility*.

Whenever you start to think about a character for a story, even a secondary character, try to sum up his or her essential characteristics in this kind of simple formula. Don't let the simplicity of this approach fool you. If you can't "capture" a character by a straightforward *emotion* vs. *emotion* equation, then you really haven't thought out the character well enough to write about him. Of course, for minor characters this isn't necessary. But it certainly is vital for the protagonist, and it can be just as important for the secondary characters, too.

With this approach, you begin to understand that the protagonist's real problem is inside his head. The basic conflict of the story, the mainspring that drives it onward, is an emotional conflict inside the mind of the protagonist. All the other conflict of the story stems from this source, as we will see in more detail in the chapters on conflict.

Kinsman's basic problem was *guilt* vs. *duty*. Years before this story took place, he killed a Russian cosmonaut in a hand-to-hand struggle during an orbital mission. It was a military mission, and both Kinsman and the Russian were military officers. Usually, when military men battle and kill each other, it's not regarded as murder.

But the cosmonaut was a woman, a fact that Kinsman did not know until he had pulled the airhose out of her helmet, suffocating her. His conscience has been screaming at him ever since, not just because he killed a fellow human being—in a situation where he might have gotten away without killing—but because it was a woman that he killed. Men can often justify murdering another man, but they have been raised to think of women as physically weaker than men. Men do not fight against women, as a rule. To kill a woman, to *murder* a woman in a hand-to-hand fight, is shocking to a man like Kinsman.

With that heavy conscience, Kinsman is locked into a two-week-long mission on the moon's surface with two other men. One of them is a priest, a symbol of conscience, a constant reminder to Kinsman that he is guilty of the sin of murder. So, even before the story actually begins, we have a very uncomfortable situation for our protagonist.

To this inner, mental problem we add an exterior, physical problem. More than one, in fact. The priest is lost, somewhere in the forbidden interior of the huge lunar crater (or ringwall) Alphonsus. The third member of the team, the astronomer Bok, is frightened to move out of the safety of their underground shelter.

This leaves Kinsman with a nasty set of problems. Where is Father Lemoyne? Is he hurt, and does he need help? Should Kinsman obey official regulations and leave the priest to his fate, or should he break the rules and try to find him?

The solution to one question, you'll notice, leads to the next one. This forms an interlocking chain of problems. The novelist Manuel Komroff chose another name for this: he called it an interlocking chain of *promises*. Because each problem or question that you put before the reader implicitly promises a solution, an answer, something intriguing and exciting to lure the reader onward. Like a western sheriff following an outlaw's trail, the reader will hunt from one problem to the next, eager to find each answer.

So you keep offering problems, asking questions, all through the story. And you never answer any question until you've raised at least one or two more, to be answered a few pages farther on. This keeps the reader turning pages anxiously, breathless to find out what happens next.

Once Kinsman finds Father Lemoyne, more problems confront him. Is the priest so near death that it would be pointless to try to rescue him? Would a rescue attempt work? Would it kill Kinsman himself? And then comes the most shocking problem of all: Father Lemoyne apparently knows about Kinsman's guilty secret. If Kinsman saves him, the priest may well reveal his secret to everyone. Kinsman will be disgraced, forced to quit his life as an astronaut, hounded by the news media, tortured in public wherever he goes.

This is where we see what the protagonist is really made of. Everything in the story points to the conclusion that Kinsman would be far better off to leave the priest in the wilderness to die. That is, if Kinsman makes a choice that we would consider to be morally wrong, it would be to his advantage. On the other hand, if he makes the morally correct choice, and tries to save the priest, it can only result in Kinsman's downfall.

Every short story should reach this kind of crisis-point. This is where you, the writer, put your protagonist—and the reader!—on the needle-sharp horns of an impossibly painful dilemma. Up to this point, you have carefully convinced the reader that your protagonist is a fine and worthwhile fellow, no matter what his shortcomings and problems may be. If you've done your work well, the reader will be imagining himself as the protagonist. I wanted you to believe that you yourself were Chet Kinsman, struggling out there on the lunar surface.

At this decision-point in the story, the writer forces the reader into an agonizing dilemma. If the protagonist chooses good instead of evil—if Kinsman saves the priest—the protagonist will surely suffer for it. If he chooses evil instead of good—if Kinsman leaves the priest to die—the protagonist will live a long and prosperous life.

In a happy-ending, upbeat story, the protagonist chooses good rather than evil. He throws to the winds all that he holds dear, for the sake of doing the morally correct thing. And instead of losing all that he held dear, he comes through the fire unhurt. Cinderella runs away from the prince, as her fairy godmother instructed her to do; yet the prince eventually finds her and they live happily ever after. Pinocchio gives up his life so that his foster-father might live, and gains not only life but humanity as a reward.

In a downbeat story, the protagonist deliberately chooses evil instead of good. He may gain everything he wanted, but he loses his soul; he becomes a bad person. In *Faust*, the protagonist literally sells his soul to the devil. He lives a long and prosperous life, but then is condemned to eternity in hell. In a more recent story, George Orwell's *Nineteen Eighty-four*, the protagonist cracks under torture and gives in to the totalitarian government of Big Brother.

He is rehabilitated and returned to normal society, but his freedom, his inner self, his soul—this has been taken away from him.

There are some stories in which the protagonist makes the right choice, and accomplishes what he set out to do, but it costs him his life. This is the classic definition of *tragedy*. In Robert A. Heinlein's science fiction short story "The Green Hills of Earth," the blind poet Reisling makes the morally correct choice—he goes into the highly radioactive engine room of the damaged spaceship and saves the ship and its passengers from total destruction. But he dies as a result. In essence, the protagonist has traded his life for the lives of all the others on the ship. He did this knowingly and willingly. There is no nobler act that a human being can perform. This makes tragedy the highest form of storytelling, when it's written well.

"Fifteen Miles" is not a tragedy, nor is it a downbeat story.

Kinsman makes the morally correct choice. He saves the priest. Sure enough, he loses everything that he wanted to keep. This is done by implication in the story, but the implication is clear: Kinsman will be grounded, never to be an astronaut or even a flier again; he will be exposed to the public, and pilloried by the press.

He won't die, of course. And in fact, he gains something of inestimable worth, something he had thought he could never find again: peace of mind. In finally letting out his secret, he loses the feelings of guilt that he had been haunted by. He has become more of a man. He realizes that he can face up to whatever the world throws at him;

he has come to terms with his own conscience. Instead of hiding, he is ready to take his punishment. He knows that the world cannot break his spirit. This is why the priest smiles at him, at the very end of the story.

The protagonist of this story has been placed in the crucible of his own emotions and put to the fire. In "Fifteen Miles" he comes out of the fire purified, stronger than he was before he entered it.

This brings up a final point to be made about character in a short story. The protagonist must *change*. What happens to him in the course of the story, no matter how short the story may be, must change him dramatically. Where he was weak, he must become strong. Where he was poor, he must become rich. Where he was evil, he must become good. (Assuming that the story is an upbeat one, of course.)

The crux of every story is the change that overcomes the protagonist. If you write a story in which the protagonist is exactly the same person at the end as he was at the beginning, you have a dull story on your hands. Find the point in his life where a crucial emotional, moral, and physical change happened to him. *That's* what you should be writing about.

5. Background: Theory

In Victorian novels, such as Thomas Hardy's *The Mayor of Casterbridge*, it wasn't unusual for the writer to take a whole chapter or more to lovingly draw in the background scenery for the story.

Modern readers won't sit still for such a slow-paced treatment, and in a short story the writer simply doesn't have the space or time to go into such detail. Yet the background can be very important to a story, and in science fiction stories the background can be vital.

For background is much more than mere scenery, or a description of the furniture in a character's house. To a large extent, the background of a story determines the mood and color of the tale. Try to imagine Poe's "Fall of the House of Usher" set in a brightly lit supermarket, with Muzak playing constantly and infants riding around in shopping carts. Or picture O. Henry's laugh-filled "The Ransom of Red Chief" taking place in Dracula's cobwebbed castle, and the surrounding Transylvanian forest!

One of the biggest problems facing the writer of a

science fiction short story is the need to create a background that is convincing without being overpowering. The writer of a contemporary story, or a historical or western or detective story, can take it for granted that the reader is familiar with most of the background details of such stories. After all, a table is a table. Modern American readers know what a stagecoach looks like; they can easily visualize in their minds the glittering chandeliers of Louis XIV's palace at Versailles; and they think they know what the inside of a jail looks like.

But what does the reader know of the ammonia seas of Titan, the largest moon of the planet Saturn? How can a reader visualize the flight deck of an interstellar passenger liner? Or the weightless recreation room, where the passengers play zero-gravity volleyball?

In each and every science fiction story, the entire background must be supplied to the reader. The writer cannot say "you know what I mean," when he mentions a laser handgun, even though he could simply use the word pistol in a western or detective story and the reader would instantly know what he meant.

This is one reason why science fiction short stories are so difficult to do well. More often, the writer will start out to produce a short story and end up with a novelet—about twenty thousand words instead of five to seven thousand—because he needed the extra wordage to draw a convincing background.

Ten thousand words or more just for the background? This is perfectly all right, *if* the background is interesting and *if* it plays an integral part in the story's development.

For example, in James Blish's famous "Surface Tension," the whole story hangs on the reader's understanding of the microscopic life forms in a small pond of water. Blish spends a good deal of time and energy showing how this microscopic world exists; he makes it fascinating in its own right—but it is also information that is vital to the unfolding of the story that Blish wants to tell.

On the other hand, there have been many science fiction stories in which the background itself has taken over the entire story, and pushed everything else into obscurity. Such stories are usually quite dull. No matter how exciting a strange world might be, people want to read about *people* and not about inanimate objects, no matter how fascinating they may be.

Of course, a really good writer can break that rule (or any other) and get away with it. John W. Campbell, Jr.'s "Twilight," for instance, was little more than the description of a dying city in the far, far future; but it was so fascinating and thought-provoking that no one has ever faulted the story for lacking human conflict and action.

There are other good stories in which no human being appears, and at first glance they seem to be nothing but background, with no plot or characters at all. But look at Ray Bradbury's "There Will Come Soft Rains." On the surface, it's the story of a completely automated house slowly falling into ruin. Look deeper. That house is itself a character, and it goes through all the phases of life (and death) that the humans did when they lived in it.

Although many writers find that they must devote about

as many words to the background of a science fiction story as they do to the main line of the story itself, there are lots of others who prefer to sketch in the background very lightly, and depend on the reader's imagination to fill in the details. These writers concentrate on the *fiction* aspects of the story—the characters and conflicts—and leave the science pretty much alone.

It's especially tempting to tell yourself that the science fiction readers already know—roughly—what a laser handgun is. Or that there have been so many science fiction stories in which starships use hyperdrive to exceed the speed of light that there's no need to give any details about such fictitious concepts.

This can be a very dangerous attitude. At the very least, it can lead to stories that are filled with jargon such as space warp, psionics, antigravs, slidewalk, and such. These may save space, but they also restrict the understanding of the story for everyone except the hard-core science fiction readers.

Worse still, they usually show that the writer has not been very original. By using the "standard" jargon of science fiction, you just might find yourself wallowing in the standard clichés, as well. It may be perfectly permissible to tread the same ground again and again in westerns or detective stories, but in science fiction, where you have the whole universe and all of time as your playground, the audience demands freshness and originality in the stories. Yes, I know, there are dull stories published that use those clichés and trot out those bits of jargon again and again.

But this is merely proof of Sturgeon's Law, coined many years ago by one of the best science fiction writers, Theodore Sturgeon:

Ninety-five percent of science fiction is crud; but then, ninety-five percent of *everything* is crud.

You want to be in the good five percent! So beware of shortcut jargon and short-circuited thinking.

This is not to say that you should spend page after page trying to describe how a thermonuclear fusion rocket works—especially since there is no such device as yet, and your description is apt to be largely phony. Sternly resist the temptation to show the reader how much science you know by piling on detailed explanations of scientific matters.

All right, then: How does a writer make an effective, fascinating background for a short story without going into excruciating detail? Here are a few simple guidelines.

First: Make every background detail *work*. That is, everything about the background should be important to the story. You don't have the room, and the reader doesn't have the time, to rhapsodize over multi-colored sunsets on a planet that has six suns. Not unless those gorgeous colors will affect the outcome of the story! If it's in the story merely for the sake of exotic detail, or simply because you enjoyed writing that paragraph, take it out. Only those background details that affect the story's development and resolution should be in your final draft.

Second: Don't try to explain how the machinery works;

just show what it does. Forty years ago, science fiction writers went into painstaking detail to show the reader that gyroscopes really could be used to maneuver a spacecraft on its way to the moon. Today such explanations are laughable, even though they're technically quite correct, because spacecraft don't use gyroscopes for attitude control; gas jets are lighter, smaller, and more reliable.

Today's reader is perfectly willing to accept that modern technology can make *anything* possible. You don't need to explain how a fusion reactor works; such an explanation would slow up the story. To convince the reader that a fusion reactor really exists, so that he will accept that part of your story, all you have to do is describe a bit of the machine's external appearance and tell the reader what it does:

The lasers that powered the fusion reactor were a lot smaller than John had expected. Small, but powerful. The reactor chamber itself was nothing more than a rounded metal dome, gleaming dully in the overhead lights. But the gauges on the power board told the real story: the reactor was turning out enough power—noiselessly—to light the whole city.

Third: Feel free to invent any new devices, to make any new scientific discoveries that you can imagine—*providing they don't contradict what is known about science today.*

This is a bit tricky, because to some extent any new scientific discovery is bound to contradict some aspect of known science. But the science fiction readers love to play The Game, as it's called. They carefully scrutinize each story, looking for scientific or technological errors. Did you ever count the shots that Hopalong Cassidy made with his six-shooter without reloading? Science fiction readers are much more meticulous than that.

For example, it's perfectly all right to do a story in which there are microscopic living creatures on Mars. None has been discovered so far, but no one can yet say that Mars is totally devoid of life. But if you try to paint these Martians as oxygen breathers, the science fiction readers will raise a howl of protest. Studies of Mars have shown conclusively that there is not enough oxygen in Mars's atmosphere to support oxygen-breathing life.

Decades ago, the science fiction audience was perfectly content to accept stories in which Mars was crisscrossed by canals, dug by intelligent Martians. Even though the best astronomical researchers stoutly maintained that the Martian canals were only optical illusions, the science fiction readers remained open-minded on the subject. Besides, Mars with canals seemed much more interesting than Mars without canals. But when spacecraft photographs showed that there are no canals on Mars, no science fiction writer could ever again do a story that had Martian canals in it. The audience would no longer accept it.

The point is that *science* fiction has some affinity with *science*. And while the science fiction audience is much more open-minded about the future than any professional scientist, it will still turn against stories that betray an ignorance or disdain of accepted scientific fact.

You can write stories in which Mars is spiderwebbed with canals. Or stories in which elephants fly, for that matter. But they will not be accepted by the science fiction audience as science fiction. They may be published, read, and enjoyed as fantasy. But if you're trying to write science fiction, you'll have to know the basics of scientific understanding. And if you break any of the fundamental laws of science, you'd better have an *excellent* explanation for it!

Fourth: You should be thoroughly familiar with the background of your story. In other words, you should write about what you know. A writer whose only contact with the Pentagon is from reading other stories or watching movies, will have a very difficult time writing convincingly about the Joint Chiefs of Staff because he hasn't found out how these people talk, or think, or act. I've seen manuscript after manuscript in which the writer is trying to deal with situations and backgrounds that he knows absolutely nothing about. Such manuscripts go from the slushpile to the return mail, usually with nothing more than a standard rejection notice on them.

No one has been to Mars, yet, although NASA has provided us all with fascinating close-up photographs of the Red Planet. But long before the *Mariner* spacecraft were even designed, Edgar Rice Burroughs and Stanley G. Weinbaum and Ray Bradbury and many others wrote stories about Mars. They weren't writing out of first-hand experience at all.

Or were they? These writers took pains to acquire as much information about Mars as they could. Then they built up a world in their own imagination that did not contradict what was known about Mars, and filled in all the unknown areas with creations of their own mind.

In a sense, each of them built a new world inside his

head, loosely based on what was known about Mars at that time. Thus Burroughs created the exotic Barsoom of John Carter, master swordsman; Weinbaum created the desert world populated by strangely nonhuman Martians; and Bradbury created a fantasy world of bone-chess cities and telepathic, very human, Martian men and women.

None of these imaginary worlds could be written about today, and still be called Mars. We know too much about Mars now; each of these imaginary worlds contradicts the pitiless advance of knowledge. But a writer can still create such imaginary worlds and place them around another star—that wouldn't contradict real-world knowledge, and the universe is vast enough to justify almost any kind of world.

This advance of knowledge is a two-edged sword. On the one hand, it makes it increasingly difficult to get away with ideas that run counter to scientific knowledge.

On the other hand, the advance of knowledge means that writers have more information on which to base stories. It's now possible to write extremely realistic stories about living and working on the moon, and any stories set on Mars nowadays will have the benefit of exact knowledge of the landscape, the weather, and all the other physical conditions of the Martian surface. We know in fine detail how nuclear reactors work, what the bottom of the ocean is like, how the double-helix molecule of DNA carries genetic information from one generation to the next.

You must write about what you know. And what you know is a combination of hard information from the world around you, plus that special interior world of imagination that is yours and yours alone—until you share it with your audience.

In short, be certain that you have the factual information you need to make your story authentic; but don't let that stifle your imagination. It's your imaginative handling of the facts that makes the difference between a dull scientific treatise and a thrilling science fiction adventure.

Fifth: This pointer is actually a corollary to the fourth one. It's important to learn the basics of science. The task is not difficult; in fact, it can be very exciting. Most science fiction writers are interested in science to some degree, although a good many of them are "turned off" by school classes in physics, chemistry, or math.

One of the best ways I know to learn about science on your own and at your own pace is to read the science books of Isaac Asimov and Arthur C. Clarke. Both these men are fine, vivid writers who can make any subject come alive. *Asimov's Guide to Science* should be on the reference shelf of every science fiction writer, along with Clarke's *Profiles of the Future*. At least!

Science is beautiful, and anyone can understand the basics of scientific thought. Poets who sing about the beauty of the stars, without understanding what makes them shine and how they were created, are missing more than half of the real splendor of the heavens.

Sixth: Equally important to the setting and scenery of a science fiction story is the care used in naming people, places, and things. Names are important; they help set the tone for a story.

The reader would have a tough time imagining a two-fisted hero named Elmer Small, but Jame Retief comes across just fine as a hero in Keith Laumer's stories. Similarly, Bubbles La Toure is hardly the name of a super-clever intelligence agent, whereas Telzey Amberdon is a marvelous name for the heroine of James Schmitz's stories.

Science fiction names should be familiar enough to be understood without fumbling over them. Yet frequently a name has to convey the alienness of a person or a locale. Too often, new writers lapse into unpronounceable collections of letters, such as Brfstklb. It's unusual, all right, but every time the reader sees it he will balk at such a name, and stop reading. The break may be momentary, but *any* break in reading a short story can be fatal.

Maps are a good place to find strange names, provided you are careful to use names that are unfamiliar, yet have an interesting ring about them. It's often useful to take a place name and give it to a person. The heroine of a novel of mine was named Altai, after the high, wild mountain chain in western China. Also, there's history to draw from: Larry Niven's character Beowulf Schaffer is fascinating even before you've met him.

One important rule of thumb about names: If a name makes the reader giggle, get rid of it. Unless it's a giggle you're after. Be ruthless about this; nothing ruins a story faster than an unintentionally humorous name.

Seventh: The final point to be made about a story's background is that it must be self-consistent. This is much more than a matter of keeping track of what time it is, and which way the wind was blowing in the last scene.

In a science fiction story, where the background forms an important element of the total story line, the background must be internally consistent. The writer cannot change winter to summer overnight because he wants a scene set on a sweltering day. More importantly, he cannot jiggle with the laws of nature to suit the needs of the story.

The archetype of this requirement is Tom Godwin's story "The Cold Equations," in which the laws of nature are themselves the background of the story. A spacecraft pilot must force a stowaway passenger out of his ship, or the ship will be too heavily loaded to reach its destination. The stowaway is a very sympathetically drawn young woman. The pilot's destination is a disease-ridden planet; his cargo is medicine to stem the epidemic. Either the girl dies or the whole planet's population dies.

Godwin could have pulled a last-minute switch and had the pilot invent some nifty device that would save both the girl and the dying people. But that would have ruined the story, dramatically. Especially since he set out to show that there are forces of nature that cannot be appeased by human desires. To quote Omar Khayyám: ". . . nor all thy Piety nor Wit/Shall lure it back to cancel half a Line/Nor all thy Tears wash out a Word of it."

When you have an explorer lost on a new planet in a sandstorm that will go on for a month, you'd better make certain that the storm doesn't stop for a full thirty days. Otherwise the reader will realize that the author has artificially helped his protagonist, and the reader will reject the story—if it gets published at all.

Backgrounds must be self-consistent in all aspects, even the mundane, undramatic ones. It makes no sense to depict a civilization that's used up all its energy-producing fuels, yet has a government that watches all the citizens over closed-circuit television. Where would the government get the fuel? Not merely the fuel to provide electricity for their electronic snooping, but the fuel that it takes to build and maintain all this widespread equipment?

And some slightly deeper thinking might lead you to the conclusion that an energy-poor civilization would not have as large a population as a modern post-industrial society. Nor would the population density be as high. A 1984-type of government would be extremely unlikely in a world that resembled the medieval subsistence farming societies of 1284 A.D.

Even though a science fiction writer can bend all the rules if he really wants to, it's best to think long and hard about it beforehand. The background of a science fiction story is so important that it often shapes the path that the story takes, just as the environment around us shapes our behavior. Pay attention to the background, and avoid the hackneyed territory that's been so overrun by mediocre stories.

Set your stories in your own unique world, guided—but not hamstrung—by known scientific information.

6. MEN OF GOOD WILL

"I had no idea," said the UN representative as they stepped through the airlock hatch, "that the United States' lunar base was so big, and so thoroughly well equipped."

"It's a big operation, all right," Colonel Patton answered, grinning slightly. His professional satisfaction showed even behind the faceplate of his pressure suit.

The pressure in the airlock equilibrated, and they squirmed out of their aluminized protective suits. Patton was big, scraping the maximum limit for space-vehicle passengers; Torgeson, the UN man, was slight, thin-haired, bespectacled and somehow bland-looking.

They stepped out of the airlock, into the corridor that ran the length of the huge plastic dome that housed Headquarters, U.S. Moonbase.

"What's behind all the doors?" Torgeson asked. His English had a slight Scandinavian twang to it. Patton found it a little irritating.

"On the right," the colonel answered, businesslike,

"are officers' quarters, galley, officers' mess, various laboratories and the headquarters staff offices. On the left are the computers."

Torgeson blinked. "You mean that half this building is taken up by computers? But why in the world . . . that is, why do you need so many? Isn't it frightfully expensive to boost them up here? I know it cost thousands of dollars for my own flight to the moon. The computers must be—"

"Frightfully expensive," Patton agreed, with feeling. "But we need them. Believe me we need them."

They walked the rest of the way down the long corridor in silence. Patton's office was at the very end of it. The colonel opened the door and ushered in the UN representative.

"A sizeable office," Torgeson said. "And a window!"

"One of the privileges of rank," Patton answered, smiling tightly. "That white antenna mast off on the horizon belongs to the Russian base."

"Ah, yes. Of course. I shall be visiting them tomorrow."

Colonel Patton nodded and gestured Torgeson to a chair as he walked behind his metal desk and sat down.

"Now then," said the colonel. "You are the first man allowed to set foot in this Moonbase who is not a security-cleared, triple-checked, native-born, Government-employed American. God knows how you got the Pentagon to okay your trip. But—now that you're here, what do you want?"

Torgeson took off his rimless glasses and fiddled with them. "I suppose the simplest answer would be the best.

The United Nations must—absolutely must—find out how and why you and the Russians have been able to live peacefully here on the moon."

Patton's mouth opened, but no words came out. He closed it with a click.

"Americans and Russians," the UN man went on, "have fired at each other from orbiting satellite vehicles. They have exchanged shots at both the North and South Poles. Career diplomats have scuffled like prizefighters in the halls of the United Nations building . . ."

"I didn't know that."

"Oh, yes. We have kept it quiet, of course. But the tensions are becoming unbearable. Everywhere on earth the two sides are armed to the teeth and on the verge of disaster. Even in space they fight. And yet, here on the moon, you and the Russians live side by side in peace. We must know how you do it!"

Patton grinned. "You came on a very appropriate day, in that case. Well let's see now . . . how to present the picture. You know that the environment here is extremely hostile: airless, low gravity . . ."

"The environment here on the moon," Torgeson objected, "is no more hostile than that of orbiting satellites. In fact, you have some gravity, solid ground, large buildings—many advantages that artificial satellites lack. Yet there has been fighting aboard the satellites—and not on the moon. Please don't waste my time with platitudes. This trip is costing the UN too much money. Tell me the truth."

Patton nodded. "I was going to. I've checked the information sent up by Earthbase: you've been cleared by the White House, the AEC, NASA, and even the Pentagon.''

"So?"

"Okay. The plain truth of the matter is—" A soft chime from a small clock on Patton's desk interrupted him. "Oh. Excuse me."

Torgeson sat back and watched as Patton carefully began clearing off all the articles on his desk: the clock, calendar, phone, IN/OUT baskets, tobacco can and pipe rack, assorted papers and reports—all neatly and quickly placed in the desk drawers. Patton then stood up, walked to the filing cabinet, and closed the metal drawers firmly.

He stood in the middle of the room, scanned the scene with apparent satisfaction, and then glanced at his wristwatch.

"Okay," he said to Torgeson. "Get down on your stomach."

"What?"

"Like this," the colonel said, and prostrated himself on the rubberized floor.

Torgeson stared at him.

"Come on! There's only a few seconds."

Patton reached up and grasped the UN man by the wrist. Unbelievingly, Torgeson got out of the chair, dropped to his hands and knees and finally flattened himself on the floor, next to the colonel.

For a second or two they stared at each other, saying nothing.

"Colonel, this is embar—"

The room exploded into a shattering volley of sounds.

Something—many somethings—ripped through the walls. The air hissed and whined above the heads of the two prostrate men. The metal desk and file cabinet rang eerily.

Torgeson squeezed his eyes shut and tried to worm into the floor. It was just like being shot at!

Abruptly it was over.

The room was quiet once again, except for a faint hissing sound. Torgeson opened his eyes and saw the colonel getting up. The door was flung open. Three sergeants rushed in, armed with patching disks and tubes of cement. They dashed around the office sealing up the several hundred holes in the walls.

Only gradually, as the sergeants carried on their fevered, wordless task, did Torgeson realize that the walls were actually a quiltwork of patches. The room must have been riddled repeatedly!

He climbed slowly to his feet. "Meteors?" he asked, with a slight squeak in his voice.

Colonel Patton grunted negatively and resumed his seat behind the desk. It was pockmarked, Torgeson noticed now. So was the file cabinet.

"The window, in case you're wondering, is bullet-proof."

Torgeson nodded and sat down.

"You see," the colonel said, "life is not as peaceful here as you think. Oh, we get along fine with the Russians—now. We've learned to live in peace. We had to."

"What were those . . . things?"

"Bullets."

"Bullets? But how—"

The sergeants finished their frenzied work, lined up at the door and saluted. Colonel Patton returned the salute and they turned as one man and left the office, closing the door quietly behind them.

"Colonel, I'm frankly bewildered."

"It's simple enough to understand. But don't feel too badly about being surprised. Only the top level of the Pentagon knows about this. And the president of course. They had to let him in on it."

"What happened?"

Colonel Patton took his pipe rack and tobacco can out of a desk drawer and began filling one of the pipes. "You see," he began, "the Russians and us, we weren't always so peaceful here on the moon. We've had our incidents and scuffles, just as you have on earth."

"Go on."

"Well—" he struck a match and puffed the pipe alight—"shortly after we set up this dome for Moonbase HQ, and the Reds set up theirs, we got into some real arguments." He waved the match out and tossed it into the open drawer.

"We're situated on the *Oceanus Procellarum,* you know. Exactly on the lunar equator. One of the biggest open spaces on this hunk of airless rock. Well, the Russians claimed they owned the whole damned *Oceanus,* since they were here first. We maintained the legal ownership was not established, since according to the UN Charter and the subsequent covenants—"

"Spare the legal details! Please, what happened?"

Patton looked slightly hurt. "Well . . . we started shooting at each other. One of their guards fired at one of our guards. They claim it was the other way 'round, of course. Anyway, within twenty minutes we were fighting a regular pitched battle, right out there between our base and theirs." He gestured toward the window.

"Can you fire guns in airless space?"

"Oh, sure. No problem at all. However, something unexpected came up."

"Oh?"

"Only a few men got hit in the battle, none of them seriously. As in all battles, most of the rounds fired were clean misses."

"So?"

Patton smiled grimly. "So one of our civilian mathematicians started doodling. We had several thousand very-high-velocity bullets fired off. In airless space. No friction, you see. And under low-gravity conditions. They went right along past their targets—"

Recognition dawned on Torgeson's face. "Oh, no!"

"That's right. They whizzed right along, skimmed over the mountain tops, thanks to the curvature of this damned short lunar horizon, and established themselves in rather eccentric satellite orbits. Every hour or so they return to perigee . . . or, rather, periluna. And every twenty-seven days, periluna is right here, where the bullets originated. The moon rotates on its axis every twenty-seven days, you see. At any rate, when they come back this way, they shoot the living hell out of our base—and the Russian base, too, of course."

"But can't you . . ."

"Do what? Can't move the base. Authorization is tied up in the Joint Chiefs of Staff, and they can't agree on where to move it to. Can't bring up any special shielding material, because that's not authorized, either. The best thing we can do is to requisition all the computers we can and try to keep track of all the bullets. Their orbits keep changing, you know, every time they go through the bases. Air friction, puncturing walls, ricochets off the furniture . . . all that keeps changing their orbits enough to keep our computers busy full time."

"My God!"

"In the meantime, we don't dare fire off any more rounds. It would overburden the computers and we'd lose track of all of 'em. Then we'd have to spend every twenty-seventh day flat on our faces for hours."

Torgeson sat in numbed silence.

"But don't worry," Patton concluded with an optimistic, professional grin. "I've got a small detail of men secretly at work on the far side of the base—where the Reds can't see—building a stone wall. That'll stop the bullets. Then we'll fix those warmongers once and for all!"

Torgeson's face went slack. The chime sounded, muffled, from inside Patton's desk.

"Better get set to flatten out again. Here comes the second volley."

7. Background: Practice

"Men of Good Will" was written as a joke; a grim joke, a technically accurate joke, but a joke nonetheless.

In "Fifteen Miles," the harsh lunar background served mainly two dramatic purposes: (1) to provide an isolated, forbidding setting for the physical ordeal that the protagonist had to go through; and (2) to provide an appropriate *symbolic* setting to mirror the protagonist's inner turmoil.

Thus the moon of "Fifteen Miles" was physically like the purgatory of Dante's *Divine Comedy*. Not that Kinsman faced punishing flames and devils. But the terraced inner walls of the crater Alphonsus form a natural analogy for the tiers of Dante's purgatory. In fact, hell itself was arranged in different levels by Dante, so it was necessary to have the priest tell Kinsman, at the end, that they were not in hell—which is eternal damnation—but in purgatory, which can be escaped after some pain.

In "Men of Good Will," the moon's airless and low-gravity environment provides the background for a bitter jest, a touch of black humor. But look at the additional background details that had to be included in the story to make the joke understandable!

We had to create a situation on earth in which World War III is imminent: Americans and Russians are firing at each other in many trouble spots around the world, and even trained diplomats—normally the politest of people —are punching each other in the UN building. The tensions are unbearable. Yet on the moon, Americans and Russians live side by side in seemingly peaceful harmony.

Then we had to show the reader that although the moon's environment is not easy or pleasant to live in, it's not the environment *per se* that has brought peace to the Americans and Russians.

Of course, it was necessary to give the reader some feeling for what life is like on the moon: hence the first few paragraphs include some sensory details—the air pressure in the airlock, the aluminized protective suits, the walk through Moonbase's main corridor. Note a couple of minor but important touches. We point out that Patton is about as big as can be allowed for spaceflight. And the name Patton itself has a ring of martial fervor, while Torgeson is described as meek and bland.

The most important bit of background painting in the first few paragraphs is to show that half of Moonbase is taken up by computers, and despite their cost, Patton maintains "with feeling" that they are vitally necessary to the base's survival.

So far the story is all background, with the possible

promise of a clash between the mild-mannered UN representative and the combative American colonel.

At this point, crazy things start to happen. They are based on a good deal of research and thinking that went into the background of the story.

Myron R. Lewis, who received a co-author's byline on this story when it first was published, had worked in ballistics tests of high-powered rifles for the U.S. Army. He worked out the details of the guns and the trajectories of the bullets. Myron is a physicist, and it was quite easy for him to calculate what muzzle velocity the guns would need to fire bullets fast enough to establish themselves in orbit around the moon. On earth, with the air resistance of our thick atmosphere and our six-times-heavier gravity, this story could never work. But on the moon, a slightly modified submachinegun could spray hundreds of bullets into lunar orbit.

The rest of the story wrote itself. It was a simple matter to look at the items on my own desk, when I wrote about the colonel clearing his desk. In fact, Colonel Patton's office is almost exactly the same as my own office of that time, except that my walls weren't rubberized fabric, and they certainly weren't riddled by bullets.

How did the writing of this story match up with the seven pointers on background given in the earlier chapter? Let's check it out.

First: The background details were each a vital element of the story. The politics, the physics, the nature of the lunar bases, even the names of the two principal characters were carefully chosen to add to the total effect of the story.

Second: We didn't bother to explain how Moonbase worked, who staffed it, or how people got to and from the moon. I doubt that lack of any of those details bothered you as you read the story. We did spend some time talking about the orbital mechanics of the bullets, because it is crucial to the story that this point get across believably. I don't think we told too much, and we made certain to leave out all the mathematics; it wasn't needed, and it would have bored most readers. (But we did the math for ourselves; at least, Myron did.)

Third: The only thing we "invented" was the overall ridiculous situation. All the science in the story could have been figured out in Isaac Newton's time.

Fourth: We certainly were familiar with the background details. Myron was the ballistics expert, we had both studied every scrap of information available about the lunar environment, and I developed the political situation as carefully as I could.

Fifth: Both of us love science. For Myron, it's a profession. For me, it's sheer fun, and the most human activity that a person can engage in. Trying to understand the universe! What could be more exciting?

Sixth: We worked out the names with care, as mentioned earlier. Also, we were careful about the place names on the moon. We needed a wide, flat plain for the site of the two bases, and the Ocean of Storms is the largest open area on the moon. Also, the choice of the name Moonbase conveys a military taste that we wanted to get across to the reader.

Seventh: I think the story is consistent. Whacky, but consistent. Of course, within thirty seconds after putting the story down you realize it's all a joke and you've been had. But the joke has a point to it: only when it is very clearly to their own self-interest do human beings refrain from warlike activities. And even when a shaky peace has been established, there will be some shortsighted people hard at work to undermine it and renew the fighting.

And that is the most important part of the background to science fiction stories. Almost every science fiction story has a philosophical point to make. Science fiction has rightfully been called "the literature of ideas." Some stories drive home their points with a bludgeon. In "Men of Good Will" we wanted to use a feather that would tickle your funnybone *and* your conscience.

Everything in the story's background was shaped for that purpose, and it's difficult for me to see any point of background information that could be removed without ruining the story's impact.

You might try that as an exercise: reread the story and see if there are any parts of the background that can be removed without destroying the story's understandability and credibility. Try the same exercise with several other stories, including some of your own. You'll be surprised at how much you can remove without hurting most stories. And perhaps you'll be equally surprised at how much you must leave in.

Remember the old newspaperman's rule of thumb: "When in doubt, throw it out." Every part of the story's background must work to enhance the story. If it doesn't, get rid of it. Learn to be ruthless with your own prose. Often the scenes you like best will have to be cut out of the story. Don't let that worry you. The result will be a tighter, cleaner story. And if the scene is really all that good, it'll start another story cooking in your mind.

8. Conflict: Theory

There's an old Italian saying that "A meal without wine is like a day without sunshine." A story without conflict is like a meal without meat.

Conflict is what makes a story. Without conflict, there is no story. You might have an interesting essay, or a lovely sketch of some scenes, or the setting and background for a story. But the story itself depends on conflict. Imagine what a drag *Romeo and Juliet* would be if the Montagues and Capulets were friendly and had no objections to a marriage between the two lovers.

The simplest form of conflict is the most obvious: action-packed fighting between two characters. This is the heart of the stereotypical western story: the good guy in the white hat shoots it out with the bad guy in the black hat. Or they fight it out with fists in the town saloon. This is called "horse opera," when the physical action is the only kind of conflict in the story.

Science fiction stories have been written along the same lines, and such stories are called "space operas." They tend to be more grandiose and larger in scale than horse operas, because the science fiction writer has the whole universe of interstellar space to work with, instead of one dusty Western town. But the pattern is the same: physical action is the mainstay of the story. Instead of cattle rustlers in black hats we have an invasion of earth by horrid alien creatures. Instead of a battle with the Indians on the prairie we have an interstellar war. But the conflict is all physical, all good guys vs. bad guys.

Back in the heyday of the pulp magazines—before World War II—space operas were the rule in science fiction, rather than the exception. The details of each story were different, of course, but the general pattern was almost invariably the same.

There was a group of Good Guys. Usually they included at least one brilliant but eccentric scientist, his beautiful daughter, and one two-fisted hero. Then there were the Bad Guys. Often they were invaders from outer space, but they could also be space pirates, interplanetary smugglers, or a dictator and his henchmen. They usually had an evil scientist in their gang, or, at the very least, the benefits of futuristic science, such as invincible weapons, hypnotic rays, invisible spaceships, or whatnot.

The Good Guys fought the Bad Guys and won. Usually they had to come up with a dazzling new invention to win, and the hero often beat the chief villain in hand-to-hand (or at least, ship-to-ship) single combat. Every reader knew from page one what the outcome would be. The thrill was in the chase, and in seeing what terrific inventions both sides would come up with.

There was no character development at all in most of these stories. The hero, the villain, the other characters were completely unchanged by all of this. There was no internal conflict in any of them. There was no real conflict between any of the characters, either, outside of the axiomatic Good Guy vs. Bad Guy fight. The entire cast of characters could go through exactly the same kind of story again in next month's issue of the magazine. And did.

Such stories seem ludicrously crude today, yet they still show up week after week in slushpiles all across the publishing industry. So let's get one thing straight right now: *Slam-bang action is not conflict.*

All right, then: what is conflict?

If you look up the word in a dictionary, you'll find several definitions. The one that pertains to writers is: "Clash or divergence of opinions, interests, etc., esp., a mental or moral struggle occasioned by incompatible desires, aims, etc."

Incompatible desires and aims. That is the kind of conflict that makes stories vitally alive. Not merely the mindless, automatic violence of Good Guys vs. Bad Guys, but the clash of desires and aims that cannot coexist. Like the thunderstorms that boil up when two massive weather systems collide, the conflict in a story must well up from the inner beings of the major characters. This conflict can come in many forms; a fist in the face or a shoot-out is the least satisfying form, because it takes the least thought to produce.

In a good story, the conflict exists at many different levels. It begins deep within the protagonist's psyche, and wells up into conflicts between the protagonist and other characters, and often—especially in science fiction—conflict between the protagonist and the forces of nature, or the strictures of society.

We saw in the chapters on character that the beginning of every story is the emotional struggle within the protagonist's mind: emotion vs. emotion, such as love vs. hate, fear vs. duty, loyalty vs. greed.

Because the writer is cramped for space and time in a short story, the protagonist must begin the story with this conflict already torturing him. Whatever it was that caused this conflict, it started before the first word of the story's opening. Sure, it may be possible to write an excellent short story in which you show the beginnings of the protagonist's agony. But as a rule, the story should be concerned with the *resolution* of the problem rather than its origins.

The short-story form is like a hundred-yard dash, compared to a cross-country race. There's no time for pacing, strategy, getting a second wind. In a short dash you go flat out, and that's all. You write about the sequence of events (or the one single event) that completely changes the protagonist's life, rather than the whole history of his existence. Novels are for telling life stories; short stories are for illuminating incidents.

So the short story begins with the protagonist's inner conflict already boiling within him. It's not necessary to blurt it out to the reader right at the outset, but the reader should quickly realize that here is a character with a problem.

Often it's the exterior manifestation of the protagonist's problem that is revealed first. In "The Second Kind of Loneliness," by George R. R. Martin, a young man has been tending a remote space station by himself for many months. The reader quickly sees that he is extremely lonely, and awaiting the relief ship that will take him back to earth. Only gradually does the reader come to realize that the man was extremely lonely even in the crowded cities of earth; he was unable to make friends, to love anyone. He would be lonely no matter where he was.

In Robert Louis Stevenson's classic, *Dr. Jekyll and Mr. Hyde,* the moral struggle between good and evil that rages within each human being is made physically real by the drug that transforms the humane Dr. Jekyll into the bestial Mr. Hyde. Stevenson is pointing out that there is a "Mr. Hyde" in all of us, which we struggle to suppress.

Most stories, though, revolve around a struggle between the protagonist and a human opponent. In science fiction, of course, neither character need be actually human. But just as the protagonist must *act like* a human being, so that the reader will feel sympathy for him, the antagonist should also be human enough so that the reader can at least understand what he (or it) is up to.

There's an important difference, incidentally, between an *antagonist* and a *villain.* It's very easy and tempting, especially for a new writer, to create a villain who is mindlessly evil. That is, a villain who does bad things simply because the story needs bad things done.

That's why I prefer to use the word *antagonist* to describe the character who clashes against the protagonist.

The antagonist doesn't realize that he's the villain of the story. He thinks he's the hero! *Nobody,* from Cain to Adolf Hitler, has ever really decided to take certain actions because they were the nasty, mean, villainous things to do. Everyone firmly believes that everything he does—no matter how horrifying—is entirely justified, necessary, perhaps even saintly.

When you have a character who is doing rotten things in a story merely for the sheer villainy of making problems for the hero, you have a weak story going. Villains, as well as heroes, must be motivated to act the way they do.

A really strong story has many tiers of conflict going in it. First is the inner struggle of the protagonist, emotion vs. emotion. Then this interior struggle is made exterior by focusing on an antagonist who attacks the protagonist precisely on his weakest point. The antagonist amplifies the protagonist's inner struggle, brings it out of his mind and into the outside world.

For example, think of Robin Hood. Hardly a science fiction tale, true, but a story with many layers of conflict.

Interestingly, the Robin Hood stories were originally spoken, not written. They are folk tales. Over the many generations before the stories were gathered together in written form, the oral story-tellers instinctively put plenty of conflict into the tales. They saw their audiences face to face and they knew what it took to keep them interested and wide-awake.

Robin's basic inner conflict is *obedience* vs. *justice.* He is an outstanding young nobleman, but his sense of right, of justice, forces him to become an outlaw. He must give up all that he holds dear and retreat into Sherwood Forest as a hunted man. His interior struggle is brought out into the exterior world of action through his chief antagonist, the Sheriff of Nottingham. The Sheriff represents law and order; Robin should be obedient to him. Yet, because the Sheriff's idea of law and order conflicts with Robin's idea of justice and right, Robin and the Sheriff are enemies.

So there are two levels of conflict going: Robin's inner struggle and his outer fight against the Sheriff. To this are added many more minor conflicts, and one overriding major conflict. The minor conflicts revolve around Robin's Merry Men, for the most part. Little John is not averse to knocking Robin into a stream, the first time they meet. Friar Tuck and many of the other outlaws often have disagreements or fights with Robin; all in good fun, of course, but there is a steady simmering of conflict that has kept readers turning the pages of Robin's story for centuries.

The story is framed in a major conflict, the struggle between King Richard the Lion Hearted and his scheming brother, Prince John. While comparatively few words in the story are devoted to this conflict, the struggle for the throne of England is actually the major force that motivates the story. We see only one small consequence of that royal struggle, the battle between Robin—a loyal follower of Richard—and the Sheriff, who supports John.

Tier upon tier, the conflicts in a good story are multi-leveled. Of course, Robin Hood is not a short story. Yet it is possible to build many layers of conflict into short stories, as well.

Consider Vonda N. McIntyre's "Of Mist, and Grass, and Sand," which received the Nebula Award from the Science Fiction Writers of America in 1974.

The protagonist is a young woman, hardly more than a girl, who is a healer. Her name is Snake. Her healing instruments include three snakes, Mist, Grass, and Sand, whom she uses as living biochemical laboratories, altering their venoms into various medicinal drugs.

Snake's inner conflict is *self* vs. *duty*. Being a healer is demanding, difficult, and a lonely life. She must travel alone across the wilderness of her planet to answer the calls of the sick.

She is called to a small, backward village where a small boy is dying of a tumor. The parents of the boy, and most of the villagers, are terrified of her and her snakes. Yet, because they cannot allow the boy to die without trying to save him, they allow her to operate on the boy. To Snake's interior conflict we now have an outer conflict: the tensions between her and the villagers. This outer conflict is also a matter of self-interest vs. duty: Snake could leave the village and its fearful, hostile people behind. But to do so would be to leave the child to die. She chooses to remain.

Treating the boy takes many, many hours. Snake begins to be attracted to one of the younger men of the village, who seems not quite as afraid of her as the others, and even tries to help her in his clumsy way. More levels of conflict: Will Snake neglect her duty because of this love interest? Will the villagers start to accept her because this man accepts her, or will they turn against him because they hate and fear Snake?

In ignorance and fear, one of the villagers kills one of the snakes, while the sick boy lies in a deathly coma. This brings out the conflict between Snake and the villagers even more sharply, and adds another level of conflict, because Snake is responsible for her "instruments." Her superiors, who taught her how to heal, will blame her for the loss. Perhaps they will stop her from practicing the healing arts.

The boy recovers and the villagers are repentant. The young man asks Snake to stay with him. She must decide between love and duty. If she stays in the village and accepts the man's love, she will be turning her back on her life as a healer. If she goes back to her superiors, they may take that life away from her and she will lose everything, including the man's love.

Snake chooses to return to her superiors, risking their anger. She leaves the man behind. The conflicts are all resolved by this choice. It doesn't really matter if her superiors prevent her from practicing the healing arts again; her choice is made. She will face whatever fate has in store for her. She did not succumb to the temptation to stay in the village and give up her profession without a struggle. She has chosen duty above self, and the reader feels that this is the morally correct choice, because if she had chosen to stay in the village, she would have given up the part of herself that makes her herself. So, by choosing duty above self, she gains her self-respect as well.

In some science fiction stories, the antagonist is not a person at all. In "Flowers for Algernon," the short story by Daniel Keyes that was later expanded into a novel and then turned into the movie *Charlie,* the antagonist is nature itself. Charlie's opponent is the universe, the blind inexorable workings of the laws of physics and chemistry.

Even though the antagonist may not be an individual character, still the protagonist must have an opponent, and that opponent must work on the basic conflict within the soul of the protagonist. In "Fifteen Miles," the harsh environment of the moon can be thought of as Kinsman's antagonist, an antagonist that forced Kinsman to bring his inner turmoil out into the open. There was much more to the story than the physical adventure problems of dragging an injured man through the wilderness to safety.

Conflict is what makes stories *move.* This is why so many science fiction stories that describe the author's idea of Utopia are so unutterably dull: in the perfect society of Utopia, there are no conflicts. No conflict means no story. You can write a lovely travelogue about some beautiful world of the future. But if you want to make the reader keep turning pages, eager to find out what happens next, you must give the story as much conflict as you can stir up.

The writer's job is to be a troublemaker! Stir up as many levels of conflict and problems for your protagonist as you can. Let one set of problems grow out of another. And never, never, NEVER solve a problem until you've raised at least two more. It's the unsolved problems that form the chain of promises that keeps the reader interested.

9. STARS, WON'T YOU HIDE ME?

O sinner-man, where are you going to run to?
O sinner-man, where are you going to run to?
O sinner-man, where are you going to run to
All on that day?

The ship was hurt, and Holman could feel its
pain. He lay fetal-like in the contoured couch,
his silvery uniform spider-webbed by dozens of
contact and probe wires connecting him to the ship so
thoroughly that it was hard to tell where his own nervous
system ended and the electronic networks of the ship
began.

Holman felt the throb of the ship's mighty engines as his
own pulse, and the gaping wounds in the generator section, where the enemy beams had struck, were searing his
flesh. Breathing was difficult, labored, even though the
ship was working hard to repair itself.

They were fleeing, he and the ship; hurtling through the
star lanes to a refuge. But where?

The main computer flashed its lights to get his attention.
Holman rubbed his eyes wearily and said:

"Okay, what is it?"

YOU HAVE NOT SELECTED A COURSE, the computer said aloud, while printing the words on its view-screen at the same time.

Holman stared at the screen. "Just away from here," he said at last. "Anyplace, as long as it's far away."

The computer blinked thoughtfully for a moment. SPECIFIC COURSE INSTRUCTION IS REQUIRED.

"What difference does it make?" Holman snapped. "It's over. Everything finished. Leave me alone."

IN LIEU OF SPECIFIC INSTRUCTIONS, IT IS NECESSARY TO TAP SUBCONSCIOUS SOURCES.

"Tap away."

The computer did just that. And if it could have been surprised, it would have been at the wishes buried deep in Holman's inner mind. But instead, it merely correlated those wishes to its single-minded purpose of the moment, and relayed a set of navigational instructions to the ship's guidance system.

> Run to the moon: O Moon, won't you hide me?
> The Lord said: O sinner-man, the moon'll be a-
> bleeding
> All on that day.

The Final Battle had been lost. On a million million planets across the galaxy-studded universe, mankind had been blasted into defeat and annihilation. The Others had returned from across the edge of the observable world, just as man had always feared. They had returned and ruthlessly exterminated the race from Earth.

It had taken eons, but time twisted strangely in a civilization of light-speed ships. Holman himself, barely thirty years old subjectively, had seen both the beginning of the ultimate war and its tragic end. He had gone from school into the military. And fighting inside a ship that could span the known universe in a few decades while he slept in cryogenic suspension, he had aged only ten years during the billions of years that the universe had ticked off in its stately, objective time-flow.

The Final Battle, from which Holman was fleeing, had been fought near an exploded galaxy billions of light-years from the Milky Way and Earth. There, with the ghastly bluish glare of uncountable shattered stars as a backdrop, the once-mighty fleets of mankind had been arrayed. Mortals and Immortals alike, men drew themselves up to face the implacable Others.

The enemy won. Not easily, but completely. Mankind was crushed totally. A few fleeting men in a few battered ships was all that remained. Even the Immortals, Holman thought wryly, had not escaped. The Others had taken special care to make certain that they were definitely killed.

So it was over.

Holman's mind pictured the blood-soaked planets he had seen during his brief, ageless lifetime of violence. His thoughts drifted back to his own homeworld, his own family: gone long, long centuries ago. Crumbled into dust by geological time or blasted suddenly by the overpowering Others. Either way, the remorseless flow of time had covered them over completely, obliterated them, in the span of a few of Holman's heartbeats.

All gone now. All the people he knew, all the planets he had seen through the ship's electroptical eyes, all of mankind . . . extinct.

He could feel the drowsiness settling upon him. The ship was accelerating to lightspeed, and the cryogenic sleep was coming. But he didn't want to fall into slumber with those thoughts of blood and terror and loss before him.

With a conscious effort, Holman focused his thoughts on the only other available subject: the outside world, the universe of galaxies. An infinitely black sky studded with islands of stars. Glowing shapes of light, spiral, ovoid, elliptical. Little smears of warmth in the hollow unending darkness; drabs of red and blue standing against the engulfing night.

One of them, he knew, was the Milky Way. Man's original home. From this distance it looked the same. Unchanged by little annoyances like the annihilation of an intelligent race of star-roamers.

He drowsed.

The ship bore onward, preceded by an invisible net of force, thousands of kilometers in radius, that scooped in the rare atoms of hydrogen drifting between the galaxies and fed them into the ship's wounded, aching generators.

Something . . . a thought. Holman stirred in the couch. A consciousness—vague, distant, alien—brushed his mind.

He opened his eyes and looked at the computer viewscreen. Blank.

"Who is it?" he asked.

A thought skittered away from him. He got the impression of other minds: simple, open, almost childish. Innocent and curious.

It's a ship.

Where is it . . . oh, yes. I can sense it now. A beautiful ship.

Holman squinted with concentration.

It's very far away. I can barely reach it.

And inside the ship . . .

It's a man. A human!

He's afraid.

He makes me feel afraid!

Holman called out, "Where are you?"

He's trying to speak.

Don't answer!

But . . .

He makes me afraid. Don't answer him. We've heard about humans!

Holman asked, "Help me."

Don't answer him and he'll go away. He's already so far off that I can barely hear him.

But he asks for help.

Yes, because he knows what is following him.

Don't answer. Don't answer!

Their thoughts slid away from his mind. Holman automatically focused the outside viewscreens, but here in the emptiness between galaxies he could find neither ship nor planet anywhere in sight. He listened again, so hard that his head started to ache. But no more voices. He was alone again, alone in the metal womb of the ship.

He knows what is following him. Their words echoed in his brain. Are the Others following me? Have they picked up my trail? They must have. They must be right behind me.

He could feel the cold perspiration start to trickle over him.

"But they can't catch me as long as I keep moving," he muttered. "Right?"

CORRECT, said the computer, flashing lights at him. AT A RELATIVISTIC VELOCITY, WITHIN LESS THAN ONE PERCENT OF LIGHTSPEED, IT IS IMPOSSIBLE FOR THIS SHIP TO BE OVERTAKEN.

"Nothing can catch me as long as I keep running."

But his mind conjured up a thought of the Immortals. Nothing could kill them . . . except the Others.

Despite himself, Holman dropped into deepsleep. His body temperature plummeted to near-zero. His heartbeat nearly stopped. And as the ship streaked at almost lightspeed, a hardly visible blur to anyone looking for it, the outside world continued to live at its own pace. Stars coalesced from gas clouds, matured, and died in explosions that fed new clouds for newer stars. Planets formed and grew mantles of air. Life took root and multiplied, evolved, built a myriad of civilizations in just as many different forms, decayed, and died away.

All while Holman slept.

Run to the sea: O sea won't you hide me?
The Lord said: O sinner-man, the sea'll be a-sinking
All on that day.

The computer woke him gently with a series of soft chimes. APPROACHING THE SOLAR SYSTEM AND

PLANET EARTH, AS INDICATED BY YOUR SUB-
CONSCIOUS COURSE INSTRUCTIONS.

Planet Earth, man's original homeworld. Holman nodded. Yes, this was where he had wanted to go. He had
never seen the Earth, never been on this side of the Milky
Way galaxy. Now he would visit the teeming nucleus of
man's doomed civilization. He would bring the news of the
awful defeat, and be on the site of mankind's birth when
the inexorable tide of extinction washed over the Earth.

He noticed, as he adjusted the outside viewscreens, that
the pain had gone.

"The generators have repaired themselves," he said.

WHILE YOU SLEPT. POWER GENERATION SYS-
TEM NOW OPERATING NORMALLY.

Holman smiled. But the smile faded as the ship
swooped closer to the solar system. He turned from the
outside viewscreens to the computer once again. "Are the
'scopes working all right?"

The computer hummed briefly, then replied. SUBSYS-
TEMS CHECK SATISFACTORY, COMPONENT
CHECK SATISFACTORY. INTEGRATED EQUIP-
MENT CHECK POSITIVE. VIEWING EQUIPMENT
FUNCTIONING NORMALLY.

Holman looked again. The sun was rushing up to meet
his gaze, but something was wrong about it. He knew deep
within him, even without having ever seen the sun this
close before, that something was wrong. The sun was
whitish and somehow stunted looking, not the full yellow
orb he had seen in film-tapes. And the Earth . . .

The ship took up a parking orbit around a planet scoured
clean of life: a blackened ball of rock, airless, waterless.

Hovering over the empty, charred ground, Holman stared at the devastation with tears in his eyes. Nothing was left. Not a brick, not a blade of grass, not a drop of water. "The Others," he whispered. "They got here first." NEGATIVE, the computer replied. CHECK OF STELLAR POSITIONS FROM EARTH REFERENCE SHOWS THAT SEVEN BILLION YEARS HAVE ELAPSED SINCE THE FINAL BATTLE.

"Seven billion . . ."

LOGIC CIRCUITS INDICATE THE SUN HAS GONE THROUGH A NOVA PHASE, A COMPLETELY NATURAL PHENOMENON UNRELATED TO ENEMY ACTION.

Holman pounded a fist on the unflinching armrest of his couch. "Why did I come here? I wasn't born on Earth. I never saw Earth before . . ."

YOUR SUBCONSCIOUS INDICATES A SUBJECTIVE IMPULSE STIRRED BY . . .

"To hell with my subconscious!" He stared out at the dead world again. "All those people . . . the cities, all the millions of years of evolution, of life. Even the oceans are gone. I never saw an ocean. Did you know that? I've traveled over half the universe and never saw an ocean."

OCEANS ARE A COMPARATIVELY RARE PHENOMENON EXISTING ON ONLY ONE OUT OF APPROXIMATELY THREE THOUSAND PLANETS.

The ship drifted outward from Earth, past a blackened Mars, a shrunken Jupiter, a ringless Saturn.

"Where do I go now?" Holman asked.

The computer stayed silent.

Run to the Lord, won't you hide me?
The Lord said: O sinner-man, you ought to been a-
    praying
All on that day.

Holman sat blankly while the ship swung out past the
orbit of Pluto and into the comet belt at the outermost
reaches of the sun's domain.

He was suddenly aware of someone watching him.

No cause for fear. I am not of the Others.

It was an utterly calm, placid voice speaking in his
mind: almost gentle, except that it was completely devoid
of emotion.

"Who are you?"

An observer. Nothing more.

"What are you doing out here? Where are you, I can't
see anything . . ."

*I have been waiting for any stray survivor of the Final
Battle to return to mankind's first home. You are the only
one to come this way, in all this time.*

"Waiting? Why?"

Holman sensed a bemused shrug, and a giant spreading
of vast wings.

*I am an observer. I have watched mankind since the
beginning. Several of my race even attempted to make contact with you from time to time. But the results were
always the same—about as useful as your attempts to communicate with insects. We are too different from each
other. We have evolved on different planes. There was no
basis for understanding between us.*

"But you watched us."

Yes. *Watched you grow strong and reach out to the stars, only to be smashed back by the Others. Watched you regain your strength, go back among the stars. But this time you were constantly on guard, wary, alert, waiting for the Others to strike once again. Watched you find civilizations that you could not comprehend, such as our own, bypass them as you spread through the galaxies. Watched you contact civilizations of your own level, that you could communicate with. You usually went to war with them.*

"And all you did was watch?"

We tried to warn you from time to time. We tried to advise you. But the warnings, the contacts, the glimpses of the future that we gave you were always ignored or derided. So you boiled out into space for the second time, and met other societies at your own level of understanding—aggressive, proud, fearful. And like the children you are, you fought endlessly.

"But the Others . . . what about them?"

They are your punishment.

"Punishment? For what? Because we fought wars?"

No. For stealing immortality.

"Stealing immortality? We worked for it. We learned how to make humans immortal. Some sort of chemicals. We were going to immortalize the whole race . . . I could've become immortal. *Immortal!* But they couldn't stand that . . . the Others. They attacked us."

He sensed a disapproving shake of the head.

"It's true," Holman insisted. "They were afraid of how powerful we would become once we were all immortal. So they attacked us while they still could. Just as they had done a million years earlier. They destroyed Earth's first interstellar civilization, and tried to finish us permanently. They even caused Ice Ages on Earth to make sure none of us would survive. But we lived through it and went back to the stars. So they hit us again. They wiped us out. Good God, for all I know I'm the last human being in the whole universe."

Your knowledge of the truth is imperfect. Mankind could have achieved immortality in time. Most races evolve that way eventually. But you were impatient. You stole immortality.

"Because we did it artificially, with chemicals. That's stealing it?"

Because the chemicals that gave you immortality came from the bodies of the race you called the Flower People. And to take the chemicals, it was necessary to kill individuals of that race.

Holman's eyes widened. "What?"

For every human made immortal, one of the Flower Folk had to die.

"We killed them? Those harmless little . . ." His voice trailed off.

To achieve racial immortality for mankind, it would have been necessary to perform racial murder on the Flower Folk.

Holman heard the words, but his mind was numb, trying to shut down tight on itself and squeeze out reality.

That is why the Others struck. That is why they had attacked you earlier, during your first expansion among the stars. You had found another race, with the same chemical of immortality. You were taking them into your laboratories and methodically murdering them. The Others stopped you then. But they took pity on you, and let a few survivors remain on Earth. They caused your Ice Ages as a kindness, to speed your development back to civilization, not to hinder you. They hoped you might evolve into a better species. But when the opportunity for immortality came your way once more, you seized it, regardless of the cost, heedless of your own ethical standards. It became necessary to extinguish you, the Others decided.

"And not a single nation in the whole universe would help us."

Why should they?

"So it's wrong for us to kill, but it's perfectly all right for the Others to exterminate us."

No one has spoken of right and wrong. I have only told you the truth.

"They're going to kill every last one of us."

There is only one of you remaining.

The words flashed through Holman. "I'm the only one . . . the last one?"

No answer.

He was alone now. Totally alone. Except for those who were following.

> Run to Satan: O Satan, won't you hide me?
> Satan said: O sinner-man, step right in
> All on that day.

Holman sat in shocked silence as the solar system shrank to a pinpoint of light and finally blended into the mighty panorama of stars that streamed across the eternal night of space. The ship raced away, sensing Holman's guilt and misery in its electronic way.

Immortality through murder, Holman repeated to himself over and over. Racial immortality through racial murder. And he had been a part of it! He had defended it, even sought immortality as his reward. He had fought his whole lifetime for it, and killed—so that he would not have to face death.

He sat there surrounded by self-repairing machinery, dressed in a silvery uniform, linked to a thousand automatic systems that fed him, kept him warm, regulated his air supply, monitored his blood flow, exercised his muscles with ultrasonic vibrators, pumped vitamins into him, merged his mind with the passionless brain of the ship, kept his body tanned and vigorous, his reflexes razor-sharp. He sat there unseeing, his eyes pinpointed on a horror that he had helped to create. Not consciously, of course. But to Holman, that was all the worse. He had fought without knowing what he was defending. Without even asking himself about it. All the marvels of man's ingenuity, all the deepest longings of the soul, focused on racial murder.

Finally he became aware of the computer's frantic buzzing and lightflashing.

"What is it?"

COURSE INSTRUCTIONS ARE REQUIRED.

"What difference does it make? Why run anymore?"
YOUR DUTY IS TO PRESERVE YOURSELF UNTIL
ORDERED TO DO OTHERWISE.

Holman heard himself laugh. "Ordered? By whom?
There's nobody left."
THAT IS AN UNPROVED ASSUMPTION.

"The war was billions of years ago," Holman said.
"It's been over for eons. Mankind died in that war. Earth
no longer exists. The sun is a white dwarf star. We're
anachronisms, you and me . . ."
THE WORD IS ATAVISM.

"The hell with the word! I want to end it. I'm tired."
IT IS TREASONABLE TO SURRENDER WHILE
STILL CAPABLE OF FIGHTING AND/OR ELUDING
THE ENEMY.

"So shoot me for treason. That's as good a way as
any."
IT IS IMPOSSIBLE FOR SYSTEMS OF THIS SHIP
TO HARM YOU.

"All right then, let's stop running. The Others will find
us soon enough once we stop. They'll know what to do."
THIS SHIP CANNOT DELIBERATELY ALLOW IT-
SELF TO FALL INTO ENEMY HANDS.

"You're disobeying me?"
THIS SHIP IS PROGRAMMED FOR MAXIMUM EF-
FECTIVENESS AGAINST THE ENEMY. A WEAPONS
SYSTEM DOES NOT SURRENDER VOLUNTARILY.

"I'm no weapons system, I'm a man, dammit!"
THIS WEAPONS SYSTEM INCLUDES A HUMAN

PILOT. IT WAS DESIGNED FOR HUMAN USE. YOU
ARE AN INTEGRAL COMPONENT OF THE SYSTEM.

"Damn you . . . I'll kill myself. Is that what you
want?"

He reached for the control panels set before him. It
would be simple enough to manually shut off the air supply, or blow open an airlock, or even set off the ship's
destruct explosives.

But Holman found that he could not move his arms. He
could not even sit up straight. He collapsed back into the
padded softness of the couch, glaring at the computer
viewscreen.

SELF-PROTECTION MECHANISMS INCLUDE THE
CAPABILITY OF PREVENTING THE HUMAN COM-
PONENT OF THE SYSTEM FROM IRRATIONAL AC-
TIONS. A series of clicks and blinks, then: IN LIEU OF
SPECIFIC COURSE INSTRUCTIONS, A RANDOM
EVASION PATTERN WILL BE RUN.

Despite his fiercest efforts, Holman felt himself dropping into deepsleep. Slowly, slowly, everything faded, and
darkness engulfed him.

> Run to the stars: O stars, won't you hide me?
> The Lord said: O sinner-man, the stars'll be a-falling
> All on that day.

Holman slept as the ship raced at near-lightspeed in an
erratic, meaningless course, looping across galaxies, dart-
ing through eons of time. When the computer's probings

of Holman's subconscious mind told it that everything was safe, it instructed the cryogenics system to reawaken the man.

He blinked, then slowly sat up.

SUBCONSCIOUS INDICATIONS SHOW THAT THE WAVE OF IRRATIONALITY HAS PASSED.

Holman said nothing.

YOU WERE SUFFERING FROM AN EMOTIONAL SHOCK.

"And now it's an emotional pain . . . a permanent, fixed, immutable disease that will kill me, sooner or later. But don't worry, I won't kill myself. I'm over that. And I won't do anything to damage you, either."

COURSE INSTRUCTIONS?

He took a deep breath. "Let's try to find some planet where the people are too young to have heard of mankind, and too innocent to worry about death."

A PRIMITIVE CIVILIZATION. THE SCANNERS CAN ONLY DETECT SUCH SOCIETIES AT EX-TREMELY CLOSE RANGE.

"Okay. We've got nothing but time."

The ship doubled back to the nearest galaxy and began a searching pattern. Holman stared at the sky, fascinated. Something strange was happening.

The viewscreens showed him the outside world, and automatically corrected the wavelength shifts caused by the ship's immense velocity. It was as though Holman were watching a speeded-up tape of cosmological evolution. Galaxies seemed to be edging into his field of view, mammoth islands of stars, sometimes coming close enough to collide. He watched the nebulous arms of a giant spiral slice silently through the open latticework of a great ovoid galaxy. He saw two spirals interpenetrate, their loose gas heating to an intense blue that finally disappeared into ultraviolet. And all the while, the once-black sky was getting brighter and brighter.

"Found anything yet?" he absently asked the computer, still staring at the outside view.

You will find no one.

Holman's whole body went rigid. No mistaking it: the Others.

No race, anywhere, will shelter you.

We will see to that.

You are alone, and you will be alone until death releases you to join your fellow men.

Their voices inside his head rang with cold fury. An implacable hatred, cosmic and eternal.

"But why me? I'm only one man. What harm can I do now?"

You are a human.

You are accursed. A race of murderers.

Your punishment is extinction.

"But I'm not an Immortal. I never even saw an Immortal. I didn't know about the Flower People, I just took orders.

Total extinction.

For all of mankind.

All.

"Judge and jury, all at once. And executioners too. All right . . . try and get me! If you're so powerful, and it means so much to you that you have to wipe out the last single man in the universe—come and get me! Just try."

You have no right to resist.

Your race is evil. All must pay with death.

You cannot escape us.

"I don't care what we've done. Understand? I don't care! Wrong, right, it doesn't matter. I didn't do anything. I won't accept your verdict for something I didn't do."

It makes no difference.

You can flee to the ends of the universe to no avail.

You have forced us to leave our time-continuum. We can never return to our homeworlds again. We have nothing to do but pursue you. Sooner or later your machinery will fail. You cannot flee us forever.

Their thoughts broke off. But Holman could still feel them, still sense them following.

"Can't flee forever," Holman repeated to himself. "Well, I can damn well try."

He looked at the outside viewscreens again, and suddenly the word *forever* took on its real meaning.

The galaxies were clustering in now, falling in together as though sliding down some titanic, invisible slope. The universe had stopped expanding eons ago, Holman now realized. Now it was contracting, pulling together again. It was all ending!

He laughed. Coming to an end. Mankind and the Others, together, coming to the ultimate and complete end of everything.

"How much longer?" he asked the computer. "How long do we have?"

The computer's lights flashed once, twice, then went dark. The viewscreen was dead.

Holman stared at the machine. He looked around the compartment. One by one the outside viewscreens were flickering, becoming static-streaked, weak, and then winking off.

"They're taking over the ship!"

With every ounce of willpower in him, Holman concentrated on the generators and engines. That was the important part, the crucial system that spelled the difference between victory and defeat. The ship had to keep moving!

He looked at the instrument panels, but their soft luminosity faded away into darkness. And now it was becoming difficult to breathe. And the heating units seemed to be stopped. Holman could feel his life-warmth ebbing away through the inert metal hull of the dying ship.

But the engines were still throbbing. The ship was still streaking across space and time, heading toward a rendezvous with the infinite.

Surrender.

In a few moments you will be dead. Give up this mad flight and die peacefully.

The ship shuddered violently. What were they doing to it now?

Surrender!

"Go to hell," Holman snapped. "While there's breath in me, I'll spend it fighting you."

You cannot escape.

But now Holman could feel warmth seeping into the ship. He could sense the painful glare outside as billions of galaxies all rushed together down to a single cataclysmic point in spacetime.

"It's almost over!" he shouted. "Almost finished. And you've lost! Mankind is still alive, despite everything you've thrown at him. All of mankind—the good and the bad, the murderers and the music, wars and cities and everything we've ever done, the whole race from the beginning of time to the end—all locked up here in my skull. And I'm still here. Do you hear me? I'm still here!" The Others were silent.

Holman could feel a majestic rumble outside the ship, like distant thunder.

"The end of the world. The end of everything and everybody. We finish in a tie. Mankind has made it right down to the final second. And if there's another universe after this one, maybe there'll be a place in it for us all over again. How's that for laughs?"

The world ended.

Not with a whimper, but a roar of triumph.

10. Conflict: Practice

"Stars, Won't You Hide Me?" began when I first heard the folk song "Sinner Man." The line from the song vibrated in my brain, and for more than ten years it kept repeating to me that it was a great line for a story title.

But a title doesn't make a story. I had the vague idea of writing a story around the basic conflict that the song suggested, a man trying to flee from his fate. The particular line about the stars suggested that the fugitive would be seeking a hiding place, or perhaps a resting place, somewhere in the infinite universe of stars and galaxies. I had spent many of my Sunday afternoons at the Fels Planetarium in Philadelphia, and I wanted to write a story that would combine the emotional conflict in the folk song with the breathtaking grandeur of the starry sky.

John Campbell, who was then the editor of *Analog,* suggested the immortality idea. It was a basic ethical conflict that he wanted someone to write about: What would the human race do if it found that it could achieve immortal-

101

ity, but only at the price of destroying another intelligent race?

That powerful conflict formed the mainspring of the story. Or at least, that's what I thought when I started writing. As it turned out, the immortality problem became almost completely a background issue—powerful, and an important motivation for everything that happens in the story, but handled strictly in the background. Perhaps for that reason, Campbell rejected the story, and it was published in another magazine.

As I started writing the story, the final idea of ending the story with the end of the entire universe hit me. It made a good resolution to a set of thorny problems, I thought. I had seen stories before then (and too many since) where the writer simply couldn't figure out how to end the tale, so he killed off the protagonist. Such stories have always seemed pointless to me, unless the protagonist's death accomplished something. In Gordon R. Dickson's "Whatever Gods There Be," for example, the protagonist sacrifices his life so that his crewmates can get safely back to Earth . . . and then some.

The basic conflict in "Stars, Won't You Hide Me?" is Holman's inner turmoil, which can be expressed as *despair* vs. *hope*. Holman is a soldier in a far-future war that spans eons of time as well as infinities of distance. He knows that the human race has lost the ultimate battle; all of humankind is doomed. He is the last man in the universe. What can he possibly hope for?

At first he gives way to mindless, numb despair. The computer that operates Holman's ship must run the craft without his conscious cooperation or help. Yet, when Holman cannot consciously think of anything to do, any place to flee to, the computer taps his subconscious memories and desires, and finds that he wants to see the Earth, the original home planet of the human race.

Although Holman consciously is giving way to despair, his subconscious mind still has desires, goals. He still has hope.

This conflict between hope and despair inside Holman's mind is made into an external conflict between the computer and the man. Time and again, Holman is ready to give up everything; he even tries to kill himself. Each time the computer prevents him from despairing and finds some reason for hope.

Holman, of course, represents the entire human race. He *is* the whole of mankind: Holman. He carries within him all the guilts and griefs of the entire race of humanity. The computer represents humankind's technology, the machines that blindly serve man, even though we sometimes wish they would leave us alone.

So we have hope vs. despair, inside Holman's mind. And man vs. machine, which brings out a new echo of the hope-despair conflict. To this we add the Others, the implacable enemies of the human race, the inexorable doom that awaits us all. The Others represent death, the end of all hope.

But before bringing out a direct confrontation between Holman and the Others, it was necessary to sharpen the focus of their enmity. Conflicts within conflicts, each building on the other. The child-like telepathic creatures who sense Holman's ship and are afraid of it; even here we have a conflict, albeit a very minor one, between these two unseen telepathic creatures. And they strike another chord of conflict: they realize that Holman is a human being, and that frightens them, both because they fear humans outright, and because they sense the Others pursuing him.

Then comes the Observer, who awakens Holman to the fact that the human race performed genocide on the harmless, beautiful Flower People, in order to give themselves immortality. Holman responds with the classic excuse of the underling: "I didn't know . . . I just took orders."

Through all this, there is also a conflict going on in the background. Holman is seeking a resting place, a hiding place, but the universe is denying him this luxury. Earth has been blasted into a cinder. He cannot rest. He is being pursued relentlessly. And even time itself is at odds with Holman. Inside his ship, which is moving at nearly the speed of light, time flows at one pace. But in the objective universe outside, time proceeds at a normal pace. Holman barely ages a few minutes while the universe goes through billions of years of objective time.

Then, with the suggestion that the universe itself is beginning to collapse, comes the confrontation with the Others.

We never see them, because to describe them in any way would rob the reader of his own imagination's vision of these ultimate demons. They make it clear to Holman that he has nothing to hope for. They will hound him until he dies. They are remorselessly committed to exterminating the last living human being.

And in this utterly inescapable doom, Holman finds hope. For if the Others are committed to destroying the human race, and Holman himself is the human race in its entirety, then all he has to do is to survive until the end of the universe—which is rushing up to meet them as the story ends.

This is Holman's triumph. No race can survive the end of the universe. If Holman still exists at the universe's final catastrophic collapse, then the Others have failed in their purpose. "We finish in a tie," Holman tells his pursuers. "Mankind has made it right down to the final second."

In the moment of death, Holman has hope. "And if there's another universe after this one, maybe there'll be a place in it for us all over again." If the universe is an eternal cycle of explosion, expansion, contraction, and collapse—as many cosmologists and theologians believe—then Holman's great discovery is that hope can *always* exist.

So, in the very end, Holman's struggle of despair against hope is decided. Despite his death, and the end of the very universe, the story is basically optimistic. A man can be robbed of everything, except hope.

We have come a long way from the simple fistfight or shoot-out, in our examination of conflict. Certainly there's nothing wrong with physical action, or military battle, as a source of conflict in a story. And in science fiction, as we've seen, the protagonist can struggle against the forces of nature or the bounds of a stifling society to generate conflict.

Yet whatever kinds of conflict you put into your stories—whether it's a karate fight or a rebellion against a dictatorship—the basic conflict must always be the struggle within the mind of the protagonist. Out of his interior conflict stem all the other conflicts of the story. If the protagonist has no inner turmoil, the story is literally gutless, and all the slam-bang action in the world will be nothing more than mindless, unnecessary violence.

11. Plot: Theory

Gordon R. Dickson is not only a fine writer, but also one of the best story "doctors" I know. Writers take their problem stories to Gordy for advice.

He was once asked, "What makes a story tick?" His answer: "The timebomb that's set to explode on the last page."

Every short story is a race against time. Something is going to happen and, whether it's good or bad, the characters and events of the story are set up to get to the time and place where that something is going to come off. Maybe it's as simple as pointing out that the king's "invisible" new clothes are actually nonexistent. Or as complex as the super nuclear device called the "doomsday machine," which literally destroys the world in Stanley Kubrick's motion picture *Dr. Strangelove*.

In most science fiction stories, the timebomb is more subtle and more complex. In Isaac Asimov's "Nightfall," it was the threat of the destruction of civilization on a planet that is always lit by its multiple suns, except for one brief night every thousand years. In Arthur C. Clarke's "The Nine Billion Names of God," it was the spooky feeling that the world might really end once the Tibetan lamas' newly installed computer had printed out all the nine billion names.

But simple or complex, subtle or bluntly obvious, the timebomb represents a *threat,* and its ticking should be loud and clear on the very first page of the story. The writer must promise to the reader that the story's protagonist is going to face an incredibly difficult problem, dangers that are overwhelming, enemies that are unbeatable, conflicts that will tear him apart.

In most stories the timebomb has several different aspects to it; the explosion promised at the end of the tale can happen at many different levels—as many different levels, in fact, as the various levels of conflict built into the story. In "Fifteen Miles" the ticking of the timebomb is a countdown that will end with: (1) either the success or failure of Kinsman's efforts to save the priest; and (2) the success or failure of his efforts to keep his secret to himself. Note that the protagonist cannot succeed in both efforts. The two conflicts also conflict with each other, placing the protagonist on the horns of an impossible dilemma.

Think about "Men of Good Will" and "Stars, Won't You Hide Me?" with an eye to understanding what the timebombs are in those stories, and on how many different levels they might explode.

The essence of creating a strong, exciting plot lies in building a powerful timebomb, and making certain that the reader can hear its ticking from the very first page—or even the first paragraph—of the story. The three aspects of short-story writing that we have already discussed—character, background, and conflict—should all be brought into focus by the plot. The protagonist must have a problem that he must solve. To solve this problem he will come into conflict with other characters and/or the environment in which he finds himself. The background of the story must contribute to the protagonist's struggle.

Some writers begin planning a story by constructing a plot, and then putting in characters, background, and conflict as necessary. For example, they start with a basic idea, such as: What would happen if the least-intelligent people of the world had larger and larger families, while the most-intelligent had fewer and fewer children? The answer turned into the late Cyril M. Kornbluth's classic, "The Marching Morons," one of the best short stories ever written in the science fiction genre. I may be entirely wrong, but it seems to me that Kornbluth got the basic idea first, worked out a plot to suit the idea, and then peopled the story with the characters, background, and conflicts that it needed.

On the other hand, it's possible to get the germ of a story idea from any point of the compass, and build the story from that starting place. Asimov's "Nightfall" began with the background of a planet where night comes only once each thousand years. My own "Stars, Won't You Hide Me?" began with the conflict suggested by a folk song. Robert A. Heinlein's "Requiem" apparently began with the character, D. D. Harriman. In "Brillo," which Harlan Ellison and I co-authored, Harlan was particularly fascinated by the character of the protagonist, Mike Polchik; the story flowed from Polchik's characterization. Many science fiction short stories seem to begin with an idea about a gimmick: an invention, a problem, an exotic new background. Then the writers work out the characters and plot to showcase the idea. Thus we get a steady succession of what are called "gimmick stories": brilliant protagonist runs into impossible problem . . . and solves it with brilliant invention, or deduction, or improvisation, or whatnot. Gimmick stories can be fun to read, but they seldom leave a lasting impression. They're like eating popcorn: it tastes good at the time, but there's very little lasting value.

And there have been so many gimmick stories in science fiction that both the readers and editors have become very critical of them. Unless the story has a truly surprising twist to it, the science fiction audience will probably figure out the ending well ahead of time, and thus the story's suspense value is ruined.

The stories that last, the stories that really stay in the readers' minds, are usually stories that have a strong interplay between a very sympathetically drawn protagonist and a powerful, overwhelming problem. The writer's task is to make the reader *care* about the protagonist. Tie him to a chair and put a timebomb at his feet; and make certain that the bomb's clock ticks loudly.

For me, as a writer, the best way to build a good plot is to begin with a strong, sympathetic protagonist and put him into action against a similarly strong antagonist.

"Strong," in this context, doesn't necessarily mean the jutting jaw, steely eyes, and bulging muscles of the typical old-time pulp magazine hero. In a novelet called "The Dueling Machine" (which I later expanded into a novel), my protagonist was a gangling, bumbling young man who could barely walk across a room without getting into trouble. His antagonist was an equally young man who had all the athletic skills and martial arts. But the protagonist had strengths that the antagonist lacked, chiefly sincerity, honesty, and a dogged, stubborn kind of heroism that could take a lot of punishment without admitting defeat.

As Kipling pointed out in his "Ballad of East and West":

> But there is neither East nor West,
> Borner, nor Breed, nor Birth,
> When two strong men stand face to face, tho'
> they come from the ends of the earth.

For most short stories, if you can place two strong characters "face to face," in conflict with each other, *they* will build the plot of the story for you. All you need to do is give them something to struggle over, and a background in which to carry on the conflict. It might be a war of chess games, as in Fritz Leiber's "The Sixty-Four Square Madhouse"; or a struggle between a lone individual and a lockstep conformist society, as in Harlan Ellison's " 'Repent, Harlequin!' Said the Ticktockman"; or a real war battle, as in Gene Wolfe's "The Blue Mouse."

In a short story there is very little room or time for a

deeply probing psychological analysis of the characters, or a gradual building up of plot and conflict. Particularly in a science fiction short story, where so much effort must be spent on making the background understandable and believable, the writer *must* open the story with that noisy timebomb. Scott W. Schumack accomplished this quite nicely in his first published story, "Persephone and Hades":

This is the way legends are born.

Twenty-three hours out of twenty-four Carver hunted her. He crept silently through the labyrinthine corridors and artificial caverns of the Necropolis, armed, wary of ambush, and above all, hating her.

In those few lines, the writer has established the protagonist, the antagonist, the background setting, and a conflict. More than that. He has dangled what's been called the "narrative hook" in front of the reader's eyes, and the reader bites on it immediately. We want to know more—who, why, where, when, how? The timebomb is ticking loud and clear in those first two paragraphs; we know it's going to go off, and we want to find out what's happening.

Every plot needs a few surprising twists and turns, of course. But even here it's best to let the characters themselves surprise you, the writer. If you have developed a set of interesting characters, people who are alive in your mind, you will find that they start to do surprising things as you write the story. They will take over their own destinies, and stubbornly resist your efforts to bend them to a preconceived plot. The villain that you wanted to capture will squeeze out of your final trap. The hero that you thought would go off in one direction will suddenly decide to do something completely different.

Let them! As long as the characters are working on the conflict-problem that they started the story with, let them do things their own way. But when they drop the original problem and begin working on something new, then you have a serious flaw in the story. Either the problem you started to write about isn't working well, or you've gotten off the track of the story completely. Then you must decide whether you're going to scrap what you've written and return to the original story-line, or to scrap the original idea and let the characters go their own way.

Next to the opening of a short story, the ending is the most critical section. The ending to a story must at the same time surprise the reader and convince him of its inevitable logic. A good short story ends like a good joke: with a snap that surprises and delights. But the ending must also be consistent with the main body of the story. You can't have the titanically powerful villain, who has the hero at his mercy, suddenly drop dead of a gratuitous heart attack. Neither can you have the hero abruptly decide that the world is too much for him, and commit suicide.

In "Men of Good Will" we had a perfectly straightforward (if somewhat daffy) story. The plot was quite simple. But it needed an ending that would make the reader say, "Gee, I never thought of that, but it's exactly what they *would* do!" So we thought up the stone wall that would eventually stop the orbiting bullets and allow the battle to be resumed.

Many new writers work very hard to pull a surprise ending out of their stories. Surprises are fine, but only when they are consistent with the rest of the story. I think that O. Henry has ruined many a promising young writer, because they read his twist endings in school and spend the rest of their writing careers trying to emulate him. Their careers are usually short, unless they outgrow the temptation to write twist endings.

I seem to be saying that surprises are fine at the end of a story, but surprise endings are dangerous. To explain: O. Henry's stories were written around the final punch line, the twist ending. Take away the ending and there is no real story. O. Henry did it masterfully, but it is essentially a gimmick, a trick, that has very limited uses. New writers should plot their stories around the main characters and their conflicts, not around a trick ending. Otherwise they produce an essentially dull, uninspired piece of work that depends entirely on the "whopper" at the very end.

Some writers like to make fairly detailed outlines of their stories, so that they know almost exactly what's going to happen, scene by scene. This makes some sense for longer works, such as novels, where the plot can get quite complicated. But for the short story, outlines can sometimes be a hindrance, rather than a help.

If the story is to flow out of the conflict between the two major characters (or the protagonist's conflict with the environment) a detailed outline might just strangle the characters' freedom of action. If the writer forces the characters to move from scene to scene, and speak the dialogue necessary for each scene exactly as outlined, the end-effect is generally a very wooden story.

Short stories usually don't have that many scenes, nor such complicated plots, that elaborate outlining is necessary. Certainly the writer must be very exact about the background details of the story, especially the science fictional elements, when the story is set elsewhere and elsewhen from here and now. And the protagonist's inner conflict must be nailed down firmly in the writer's mind before the first words are set on paper. But more often than not, a detailed outline of the plot stultifies the story. If you know your characters and their conflicts, you should let them write the story for you. Only if you find yourself drifting hopelessly at sea, should you make a detailed outline for plotting purposes.

In writing stories of any length, the most important thing to keep in mind is "show, don't tell." This is especially true in the short story.

The moment you break the flow of the story's action to explain things to the reader, you run the risk of losing the reader. All of a sudden, instead of being *in* the story, living the role of the protagonist, the reader is listening to you lecturing him. No matter how important the information you want to get across to him, the reader is immediately reminded that he's *reading*, rather than living in the story. It's a risk that you should never run, if you can avoid it. Never give the reader an opportunity to look up from the page.

If you find it necessary to explain the eighteen-century-long history of the Terran Confederation, find some way to have the characters do it for you. And not by having them discuss it! Putting dull lectures into dialogue form doesn't stop them from being dull lectures. If the story absolutely will not work without all that background history, you must *personify* the information in a character, and have that character's actions *show* the reader what you want him to learn.

In ninety-nine cases out of a hundred, all that background information can be chopped out of the story with no loss at all. The reader generally doesn't need or want long treatises of background information. It's important that the writer know this information, because it will shape the actions of the story's characters. But in almost every case, the story can get along perfectly well without the lecture, and the reader will be much happier without it.

If you are in doubt about this point, take a story you have written that has a large amount of background explanation in it, and remove the explanations. See for yourself if the story doesn't move more swiftly and keep your interest better. Of course, some of the characters' actions and motivations may be unexplained; but you will probably find a way to explain them through action, instead of lecturing.

An important rule of thumb, when it comes to imparting background information, is never to allow the characters to tell each other anything that they already know. It's always tempting to explain things to the reader by using this technique, but it's always a mistake.

"Why John," he said, "you remember how the expedition team got across Endless Swamp, don't you?"

"Of course I do," John replied. "They glued their snowshoes together to make a raft, and then . . ."

If you feel it absolutely necessary to get that particular point across to the reader, *do it through action*. Without even raising the question of the Endless Swamp Exploration Team, have John glance at a battered set of glued-together snowshoes hanging on the wall of his host's den. And even then, don't do it at all unless you're going to *use* those glued-together snowshoes later in the story. Like all background information, if it doesn't contribute to the story, throw it out.

Good writers are good plotters, although they seldom let a preconceived plot take such complete command of a story that it stiffens the characters and forces them into artificial situations. Mark Twain, one of the best writers America has produced, penned a marvelous essay about writing, titled "Fenimore Cooper's Literary Offenses." It is funny, pointed, and contains more good advice about writing than any other sixteen pages in the English language.

Two important points that Twain raises about story construction are: "That a tale shall accomplish something and arrive somewhere. [And] . . . that the episodes of a tale shall be necessary parts of the tale and shall help to develop it."

In other words, a story should have a beginning, a middle, and an end. It's distressingly true that many, *many*

slushpile stories lack such organization. They wander aim-
lessly, with no clear-cut purpose or conflict to give them
shape and meaning. If you set your timebomb to go off at
the end of the story, and start it ticking on the first page,
then almost inevitably the story will be a record of the protagonist's attempts to prevent the explosion from wrecking
his life. The story will "accomplish something and arrive
somewhere," never fear.

All the scenes and events in the story must play a vital
role in developing the story. You don't have time or room
to spend the first few pages describing the hero's family
background, or the geological forces on the newly discovered planet Whatsit. Start the clock ticking! Delete every
scene and every line of dialogue that doesn't contain a tick
of the timebomb's clock in it! Be ruthless with your own
prose. It's painful, well I know; but it's necessary.

As the plot develops, the story must *move*. That is, it
must progress from the beginning, through the middle, to
the end. The protagonist must learn things, grow, and
change. The reader must discover something new and,
hopefully, something delightfully interesting (or frightening)
on every page.

Many new writers (and even some old hands, alas) con-
fuse *motion* with *movement*. That is, they whiz the protagonist out of his office, down a conveyor-belt slidewalk,
into a jet helicopter, out to the space port, onto a shuttle
rocket, and from there to the space station and finally into
the antagonist's antigravity-driven starship—all in the
name of movement. But if nothing is happening except a

recitation of various modes of transportation, the story isn't moving at all!

The characters can run breathlessly in circles for page after page while the story stands still. The reader watches, bemused, as doors open and slam, engines roar, seatbelts get fastened—and nothing happens. If there's too much of this in a story the reader will put it down and go off to the medicine chest for some Dramamine. Just as physical action is not necessarily conflict, physical motion is not necessarily movement.

A story moves when the protagonist (and the reader) makes a new discovery. All the rest is busywork.

Final point: A really good writer convinces the reader that the protagonist had a rich and busy life before the story began, and will continue to do so after the last page of the story has been finished. In other words, the plot should be arranged so that the reader gets the feeling that this character is really *alive;* his life didn't begin on page one and end on page last; he encompasses much more than merely the events of this one short story. Perhaps we shall meet him again, someday.

Of course, if the protagonist dies at the end of the story the reader can't expect to find him again. But there should be some character mourning for the protagonist that *will* live on. A sense of continuity is a subtle, but extremely powerful, method for convincing the reader that the story is really true.

12. THE SHINING ONES

Johnny Donato lay flat on his belly in the scraggly grass and watched the strangers' ship carefully.

It was resting on the floor of the desert, shining and shimmering in the bright New Mexico sunlight. The ship was huge and round like a golden ball, like the sun itself. It touched the ground as lightly as a helium-filled balloon. In fact, Johnny wasn't sure that it really did touch the ground at all.

He squinted his eyes, but he still couldn't tell if the ship was really in contact with the sandy desert flatland. It cast no shadow, and it seemed to glow from some energies hidden inside itself. Again, it reminded Johnny of the sun.

But these people didn't come from anywhere near our sun, Johnny knew. *They come from a world of a different star.*

He pictured in his mind how small and dim the stars look at night. Then he glanced at the powerful glare of the sun. *How far away the stars must be!* And these strangers

have travelled all that distance to come here. To Earth. To
New Mexico. To this spot in the desert.

Johnny knew he should feel excited. Or maybe scared.
But all he felt right now was curious. And hot. The sun
was beating down on the rocky ledge where he lay watching, baking his bare arms and legs. He was used to the
desert sun. It never bothered him.

But today something was burning inside Johnny. At first
he thought it might be the sickness. Sometimes it made
him feel hot and weak. But no, that wasn't it. He had the
sickness, there was nothing anyone could do about that.
But it didn't make him feel this way.

This thing inside him was something he had never felt
before. Maybe it was the same kind of thing that made his
father yell in fury, ever since he had been laid off from his
job. Anger was part of it, and maybe shame, too. But
there was something else, something Johnny couldn't put a
name to.

So he lay there flat on his belly, wondering about himself and the strange ship from the stars. He waited pa-
tiently, like his Apache friends would, while the sun
climbed higher in the bright blue sky and the day grew
hotter and hotter.

The ship had landed three days earlier. *Landed* was really the wrong word. It had touched down as gently as a
cloud drifts against the tops of the mountains. Sergeant
Warner had seen it. He just happened to be driving down
the main highway in his State Police cruiser when the ship
appeared. He nearly drove into the roadside culvert, staring at the ship instead of watching his driving.

Before the sun went down that day, hundreds of Army trucks and tanks had poured down the highway, swirling up clouds of dust that could be seen even from Johnny's house in Albuquerque, miles away. They surrounded the strange ship and let no one come near it.

Johnny could see them now, a ring of steel and guns. Soldiers paced slowly between the tanks, with automatic rifles slung over their shoulders. Pretending that he was an Apache warrior, Johnny thought about how foolish the Army was to make the young soldiers walk around in the heat instead of allowing them to sit in the shade. He knew that the soldiers were sweating and grumbling and cursing the heat. As if that would make it cooler. They even wore their steel helmets; a good way to fry their brains.

Each day since the ship had landed, exactly when the sun was highest in the sky, three strangers would step out of the ship. At least, that's what the people were saying back in town. The newspapers carried no word of the strangers, except front-page complaints that the Army wouldn't let news reporters or television camera crews anywhere near the star ship.

The three strangers came out of their ship each day, for a few minutes. Johnny wanted to talk to them. Maybe— just maybe—they could cure his sickness. All the doctors he had ever seen just shook their heads and said that nothing could be done. Johnny would never live to be a full-grown man. But these strangers, if they really came from another world, a distant star, they might know how to cure a disease that no doctor on Earth could cure.

Johnny could feel his heart racing as he thought about it.

He forced himself to stay calm. *Before you can get cured,* he told himself, *you've got to talk to the strangers. And before you can do that, you've got to sneak past all those soldiers.*

A smear of dust on the highway caught his eye. It was a State Police car, heading toward the Army camp. Sergeant Warner, most likely. Johnny figured that his mother had realized by now he had run away, and had called the police to find him. So he had another problem: avoid getting found by the police.

He turned back to look at the ship again. Suddenly his breath caught in his throat. The three strangers were standing in front of the ship. Without opening a hatch, without any motion at all. They were just *there,* as suddenly as the blink of an eye.

They were tall and slim and graceful, dressed in simple-looking coveralls that seemed to glow, just like their ship.

And they cast no shadows!

2

The strangers stood there for several minutes. A half-dozen people went out toward them, two in Army uniforms, the others in civilian clothes. After a few minutes the strangers disappeared. Just like that. Gone. The six men seemed just as stunned as Johnny felt. They milled around for a few moments, as if trying to figure out where the strangers had gone to. Then they slowly walked back toward the trucks and tanks and other soldiers.

Johnny pushed himself back down from the edge of the hill he was on. He sat up, safely out of view of the soldiers and police, and checked his supplies. A canteen full of water, a leather sack that held two quickly made sandwiches and a couple of oranges. He felt inside the sack to see if there was anything else. Nothing except the wadded-up remains of the plastic wrap that had been around the other two sandwiches he had eaten earlier. The only other thing he had brought with him was a blanket to keep himself warm during the chill desert night.

There wasn't much shade, and the sun was getting really fierce. Johnny got to his feet and walked slowly to a clump of bushes that surrounded a stunted dead tree. He sat down and leaned his back against the shady side of the tree trunk.

For a moment he thought about his parents.

His mother was probably worried sick by now. Johnny often got up early and left the house before she was awake, but he always made sure to be back by lunchtime. His father would be angry. But he was always angry nowadays—most of the time it was about losing his job. But Johnny knew that what was really bugging his father was Johnny's own sickness.

Johnny remembered Dr. Pemberton's round red face, which was normally so cheerful. But Dr. Pemberton shook his head grimly when he told Johnny's father:

"It's foolish for you to spend what little money you have, John. Leukemia is incurable. You could send the boy to one of the research centers, and they'll try out some of the new treatments on him. But it won't help him. There is no cure."

Johnny hadn't been supposed to hear that. The door between the examination room where he was sitting and Dr. Pemberton's office had been open only a crack. It was enough for his keen ears, though.

Johnny's father sounded stunned. "But . . . he looks fine. And he says he feels okay."

"I know." Dr. Pemberton's voice sounded as heavy as his roundly overweight body. "The brutal truth, however, is that he has less than a year to live. The disease is very advanced. Luckily, for most of the time he'll feel fine. But towards the end . . ."

"These research centers," Johnny's father said, his voice starting to crack. "The scientists are always coming up with new vaccines . . ."

Johnny had never heard his father sound like that: like a little boy who had been caught stealing or something, and was begging for a chance to escape getting punished.

"You can send him to a research center," Dr. Pemberton said, slowly. "They'll use him to learn more about the disease. But there's no cure in sight, John. Not this year. Or next. And that's all the time he has."

And then Johnny heard something he had never heard before in his whole life: his father was crying.

They didn't tell him.

He rode back home with his father, and the next morning his mother looked as if she had been crying all night. But they never said a word to him about it. And he never told them that he knew.

Maybe it would have been different if he had a brother or sister to talk to. And he couldn't tell the kids at school, or his friends around the neighborhood. What do you say?

"Hey there, Nicko . . . I'm going to die around Christmas sometime."

No. Johnny kept silent, like the Apache he often dreamed he was. He played less and less with his friends, spent more and more of his time alone.

And then the ship came.

It had to *mean* something. A ship from another star doesn't just plop down practically in your back yard by accident.

Why did the strangers come to Earth?

No one knew. And Johnny didn't really care. All he wanted was a chance to talk to them, to get them to cure him. Maybe—who knew?—maybe they were here to find him and cure him!

He dozed off, sitting there against the tree. The heat was sizzling, there was no breeze at all, and nothing for Johnny to do until darkness. With his mind buzzing and jumbling a million thoughts together, his eyes drooped shut and he fell asleep.

"Johnny Donato!"

The voice was like a crack of thunder. Johnny snapped awake, so surprised that he didn't even think of being scared.

"Johnny Donato! This is Sergeant Warner. We know you're around here, so come out from wherever you're hiding."

Johnny flopped over on his stomach and peered around. He was pretty well hidden by the bushes that surrounded the tree. Looking carefully in all directions, he couldn't see Sergeant Warner or anyone else.

"Johnny Donato!" the voice repeated. "This is Sergeant Warner . . ."

Only now the voice seemed to be coming from farther away. Johnny realized that the State Police sergeant was speaking into an electric bullhorn.

Very slowly, Johnny crawled on his belly up to the top of the little hill. He made certain to stay low and keep in the scraggly grass.

Off to his right a few hundred yards was Sergeant Warner, slowly walking across the hot sandy ground. His hat was pushed back on his head, pools of sweat stained his shirt. He held the bullhorn up to his mouth, so that Johnny couldn't really see his face at all. The sergeant's mirror-shiny sunglasses hid the top half of his face.

Moving still farther away, the sergeant yelled into his bullhorn, "Now listen Johnny. Your mother's scared half out of her mind. And your father doesn't even know you've run away—he's still downtown, hasn't come home yet. You come out now, you hear? It's hot out here, and I'm getting mighty unhappy about you."

Johnny almost laughed out loud. *What are you going to do, kill me?*

"Dammit, Johnny, I know you're around here! Now, do I have to call in other cars and the helicopter, just to find one stubborn boy?"

Helicopters! Johnny frowned. He had no doubts that he could hide from a dozen police cars and the men in them. But helicopters were something else.

He crawled back to the bushes and the dead tree and started scooping up loose sand with his bare hands. Pretty soon he was puffing and sweaty. But finally he had a shallow trench that was long enough to lie in.

He got into the trench and pulled his food pouch and canteen in with him. Then he spread the blanket over himself. By sitting up and leaning foward, he could reach a few small stones. He put them on the lower corners of the blanket to anchor them down. Then he lay down and pulled the blanket over him.

The blanket was brown, and probably wouldn't be spotted from a helicopter. Lying there under it, staring at the fuzzy brightness two inches over his nose, Johnny told himself he was an Apache hiding out from the Army.

It was almost true.

It got very hot in Johnny's hideout. Time seemed to drag endlessly. The air became stifling; Johnny could hardly breathe. Once he thought he heard the drone of a helicopter, but it was far off in the distance. Maybe it was just his imagination.

He drifted off to sleep again.

Voices woke him up once more. More than one voice this time, and he didn't recognize who was talking. But they were very close by—they weren't using a bullhorn or calling out to him.

"Are you really sure he's out here?"

"Where else would a runaway kid go? His mother says he hasn't talked about anything but that weirdo ship for the past three days."

"Well, it's a big desert. We're never going to find him standing around here jabbering."

"I got an idea." The voices started to get fainter, as if the men were walking away.

"Yeah? What is it?"

Johnny stayed very still and strained his ears to hear them.

"Those Army guys got all sorts of fancy electronic stuff. Why don't we use them instead of walking around here frying our brains?"

"They had some of that stuff on the helicopter, didn't they?"

The voices were getting fainter and fainter.

"Yeah—but instead of trying to find a needle in a haystack, we ought to play it smart."

"What do you mean?"

Johnny wanted to sit up, to hear them better. But he didn't dare move.

"Why not set up the Army's fancy stuff and point it at the ship? That's where the kid wants to go. Instead of searching the whole damned desert for him . . ."

"I get it!" the other voice said. "Make the ship the bait in a mousetrap."

"Right. That's the way to get him."

They both laughed.

And Johnny, lying quite still in his hideaway, began to know how a starving mouse must feel.

3

After a long, hot, sweaty time Johnny couldn't hear any more voices or helicopter engines. And as he stared tiredly at the blanket over him, it seemed that the daylight was growing dimmer.

Must be close to sundown, he thought.

Despite his worked-up nerves, he fell asleep again. By the time he woke up, it was dark.

He sat up and let the blanket fall off to one side of his dugout shelter. Already it was getting cold.

But Johnny smiled.

If they're going to have all their sensors looking in toward the ship, he told himself, *that means nobody's out here. It ought to be easy to get into the Army camp and hide there. Maybe I can find someplace warm. And food!*

But another part of his mind asked, *And what then? How are you going to get from there to the ship and the strangers?*

"I'll cross that bridge when I come to it," Johnny whispered to himself.

Clutching the blanket around his shoulders, for warmth in the chilly desert night wind, Johnny crept up to the top of the hill once more.

The Army tanks and trucks were still out there. A few tents had been set up, and there were lights strung out everywhere. It almost looked like a shopping center decorated for the Christmas season, there were so many lights and people milling around.

But the lights were glaring white, not the many colors of the holidays. And the people were soldiers. And the decorations were guns, cannon, radar antennas, lasers—all pointed inward at the strangers' ship.

The ship itself was what made everything look like Christmas, Johnny decided. It stood in the middle of everything, glowing and golden like a cheerful tree ornament.

Johnny stared at it for a long time. Then he found his gaze floating upward, to the stars. In the clear cold night of the desert, the stars gleamed and winked like thousands of jewels: red, blue, white. The hazy swarm of the Milky Way swung across the sky. Johnny knew there were billions of stars in the heavens, hundreds of billions, so many stars that they were uncountable.

"That ship came from one of them," he whispered to himself. "Which one?"

The wind moaned and sent a shiver of cold through him, despite his blanket.

Slowly, quietly, carefully, he got up and started walking down the hill toward the Army camp. He stayed in the shadows, away from the lights, and circled around the trucks and tanks. He was looking for an opening, a dark place where there was no one sitting around or standing guard, a place where he could slip in and maybe hide inside one of the trucks.

I wonder what the inside of a tank is like? he asked himself. Then he shook his head, as if to drive away such childish thoughts. He was an Apache warrior, he told himself, sneaking up on the Army camp.

He got close enough to hear soldiers talking and laughing among themselves. But still he stayed out in the darkness. He ignored the wind and cold, just pulled the blanket more tightly over his thin shoulders as he circled the camp. Off beyond the trucks, he could catch the warm yellow glow of the strangers' ship. It looked inviting and friendly.

And then there was an opening! A slice of shadow that cut between pools of light. Johnny froze in his tracks and examined the spot carefully, squatting down on his heels to make himself as small and undetectable as possible.

There were four tents set up in a row, with their backs facing Johnny. On one side of them was a group of parked trucks and jeeps. Metal poles with lights on them brightened that area. On the other side of the tents were some big trailer vans, with all sorts of antennas poking out of their roofs. That area was well-lit too.

But the narrow lanes between the tents were dark with shadow. And Johnny could see no one around them. There were no lights showing from inside the tents, either.

Johnny hesitated only a moment or two. Then he quickly stepped up to the rear of one of the tents, poked his head around its corner and found no one in sight. So he ducked into the lane between the tents.

Flattening himself against the tent's vinyl wall, Johnny listened for sounds of danger. Nothing except the distant rush of the wind and the pounding of his own heart. It was dark where he was standing. The area seemed to be deserted.

He stayed there for what seemed like hours. His mind was saying that this was a safe place to hide. But his stomach was telling him that there might be some food inside the tents.

Yeah, and there might be some people inside there, too, Johnny thought.

His stomach won the argument.

Johnny crept around toward the front of the tent. This

area was still pretty well lit from the lamps over by the trucks and vans. Peeking around the tent's corner, Johnny could see plenty of soldiers sitting in front of the parking areas, on the ground alongside their vehicles, eating food that steamed and somehow looked delicious, even from this distance. Johnny sniffed at the night air and thought he caught a trace of something filled with meat and bubbling juices.

Licking his lips, he slipped around the front of the tent and ducked inside.

It was dark, but enough light filtered through from the outside for Johnny to see that the tent was really a workroom of some sort. Two long tables ran the length of the tent. There were papers stacked at one end of one table, with a metal weight holding them in place. All sorts of instruments and gadgets were sitting on the tables: microscopes, cameras, something that looked sort of like a computer, other things that Johnny couldn't figure out at all.

None of it was food.

Frowning, Johnny went back to the tent's entrance. His stomach was growling now, complaining about being empty too long.

He pushed the tent flap back half an inch and peered outside. A group of men were walking in his direction. Four of them. One wore a soldier's uniform and had a big pistol strapped to his hip. The others wore ordinary clothes: slacks, Windbreaker jackets. One of them was smoking a pipe—or rather, he was waving it in his hand as he talked, swinging the pipe back and forth and pointing its stem at the glowing ship, then back at the other three men.

Johnny knew that if he stepped outside the tent now they would see him as clearly as anything.

Then he realized that the situation was even worse. They were heading straight for this tent!

4

There wasn't any time to be scared. Johnny let the tent flap drop back into place and dived under one of the tables. No place else to hide.

He crawled into the farthest corner of the tent, under the table, and huddled there with his knees pulled up tight against his nose and the blanket wrapped around him.

Sure enough, the voices marched straight up to the tent and the lights flicked on.

"You'd better get some sleep, Ed. No sense staying up all night again."

"Yeah, I will. Just want to go over the tapes from this afternoon one more time."

"Might as well go to sleep, for all the good *that's* going to do you."

"I know. Well . . . see you tomorrow."

"G'night."

From underneath the table, Johnny saw a pair of desert-booted feet walk into the tent. The man, whoever it was, wore striped slacks. He wasn't a soldier, or a policeman, and that let Johnny breathe a little easier.

"You know you'll have to go back home again, don't you?"

"I guess so."

"Your parents are probably worried. I thought I heard one of the State Troopers say that you were ill?"

Johnny nodded.

"Want to talk about it?"

Johnny turned his attention back to the tray of food. "No."

Gene gave a little one-shouldered shrug. "Okay. As long as you don't need any medicine right away, or anything like that."

Looking up again, Johnny asked, "Are you a scientist?"

"Sort of. I'm a linguist."

"Huh?"

"I study languages. The Army came and got me out of the university so I could help them understand the language the aliens speak."

"Aliens?"

"The men from the ship."

"Oh. Aliens—that's what you call them?"

"Right."

"Can you understand what they're saying?"

Gene grinned again, but this time it wasn't a happy expression. "Can't understand anything," he said.

"Nothing?" Johnny felt suddenly alarmed. "Why not?"

"Because the aliens haven't said anything to us."

"Huh?"

With a shake of his head, Gene said, "They just come out every day at high noon, stand there for a few minutes while we talk at them, and then pop back into their ship. I don't think they're listening to us at all. In fact, I don't think they're even *looking* at us. It's like they don't even know we're here!"

5

Gene let Johnny listen to the tapes of their attempts to talk to the aliens.

With the big padded stereo earphones clamped to his head, Johnny could hear the Army officers speaking, and another man that Gene said was a scientist from Washington. He could hear the wind, and a soft whistling sound, like the steady note of a telephone that's been left off the hook for too long. But no sounds at all from the aliens. No words of any kind, in any language.

Gene helped take the earphones off Johnny's head.

"They haven't said anything at all?"

"Nothing," Gene answered, clicking off the tape recorder. "The only sound to come from them is that sort of whistling thing—and that's coming from the ship. Some of the Army engineers think it's a power generator of some sort."

"Then we can't talk with them," Johnny suddenly felt very tired and defeated.

"We can talk *to* them," Gene said, "but I'm not even

certain that they hear us. It's . . . it's pretty weird. They seem to look right through us—as if we're pictures hanging on a wall.''

"Or rocks or grass or something.''

"Right!'' Gene looked impressed. "Like we're a part of the scenery, nothing special, nothing you'd want to talk to.''

Something in Johnny was churning, trying to break loose. He felt tears forming in his eyes. "Then how can I tell them . . .''

"Tell them what?'' Gene asked.

Johnny fought down his feelings. "Nothing,'' he said. "It's nothing.''

Gene came over and put a hand on Johnny's shoulder. "So you're going to tough it out, huh?''

"What do you mean?''

Smiling, Gene answered, "Listen kid. Nobody runs away from home and sneaks into an Army camp just for fun. At first I thought you were just curious about the aliens. But now . . . looks to me as if you've got something pretty big on your mind.''

Johnny didn't reply, but—strangely—he felt safe with this man. He wasn't afraid of him anymore.

"So stay quiet,'' Gene went on. "It's *your* problem, whatever it is, and you've got a right to tell me to keep my nose out of it.''

"You're going to tell the State Troopers I'm here?''

Instead of answering, Gene leaned against the table's edge and said, "Listen. When I was just about your age I ran away from home for the first time. That was in Cleveland. It was winter and there was a lot of snow. Damned cold, too. Now, you'd think that whatever made me leave home and freeze my backside in the snow for two days and nights—you'd think it was something pretty important, wouldn't you?"

"Wasn't it?"

Gene laughed out loud. "I don't know! I can't for the life of me remember what it was! It was awfully important to me then, of course. But now it's nothing, nowhere."

Johnny wanted to laugh with him, but he couldn't. "My problem's different."

"Yeah, I guess so," Gene said. But he was still smiling.

"I'm going to be dead before the year's over," Johnny said.

Gene's smile vanished. "What?"

Johnny told him the whole story. Gene asked several questions, looked doubtful for a while, but at last simply stood there looking very grave.

"That *is* tough," he said, at last.

"So I thought maybe the strangers—the aliens, that is—might do something, maybe cure it . . ." Johnny's voice trailed off.

"I see," Gene said. And there was real pain in his voice. "And we can't even get them to notice us, let alone talk with us."

"I guess it's hopeless then."

Gene suddenly straightened up. "No. Why should we give up? There must be something we can do!"

"Like what?" Johnny asked.

Gene rubbed a hand across his chin. It was dark with stubbly beard. "Well . . . maybe they *do* understand us and just don't care. Maybe they're just here sightseeing, or doing some scientific exploring. Maybe they think of us like we think of animals in a zoo, or cows in a field—"

"But we're not animals!" Johnny said.

"Yeah? Imagine how we must seem to them." Gene began to pace down the length of the table. "They've travelled across lightyears—billions on billions of miles—to get here. Their ship, their brains, their minds must be thousands of years ahead of our own. We're probably no more interesting to them than apes in a zoo."

"Then why . . ."

"Wait a minute," Gene said. "Maybe they're not interested in us—but so far they've only seen adults, men, soldiers mostly. Suppose we show them a child, *you*, and make it clear to them that you're going to die."

"How are you going to get that across to them?"

"I don't know," Gene admitted. "Maybe they don't even understand what death is. Maybe they're so far ahead of us that they live for thousands of years—or they might even be immortal!"

Then he turned to look back at Johnny. "But I've had the feeling ever since the first time we tried to talk to them that they understand every word we say. They just don't *care.*"

"And you think they'll care about me?"

"It's worth a try. Nothing else we've done has worked. Maybe this will."

6

Gene took Johnny to a tent that had cots and warm Army blankets.

"You get some sleep; you must be tired," he said. "I'll let the State Police know you're okay."

Johnny could feel himself falling asleep, even though he was only standing next to one of the cots.

"Do you want to talk to your parents? We can set up a radio-phone . . ."

"Later," Johnny said. "As long as they know I'm okay—I don't want to hassle with them until after we've talked to the aliens."

Gene nodded and left the tent. Johnny sat on the cot, kicked off his boots, and was asleep by the time he had stretched out and pulled the blanket up to his chin.

Gene brought him breakfast on a tray the next morning. But as soon as Johnny had finished eating and pulled his boots back on, Gene led him out to one of the big vans.

"General Hackett isn't too sure he likes our idea," Gene said as they walked up to the tan-colored van. It was like a civilian camper, only much bigger. Two soldiers stood guard by its main door, with rifles slung over their shoulders. It was already hot and bright on the desert, even though the sun had hardly climbed above the distant mountains.

The alien star ship still hung in the middle of the camp circle, glowing warmly and barely touching the ground. For a wild instant, Johnny thought of it as a bright beach ball being balanced on a seal's nose.

Inside, the van's air conditioning was turned up so high that it made Johnny shiver.

But General Hackett was sweating. He sat squeezed behind a table, a heavy, fat-cheeked man with a black little cigar stuck in the corner of his mouth. It was not lit, but Johnny could smell its sour odor. Sitting around the little table in the van's main compartment were Sergeant Warner of the State Police, several civilians, and two other Army officers, both colonels.

There were two open chairs. Johnny and Gene slid into them.

"I don't like it," General Hackett said, shaking his head. "The whole world's going nuts over these weirdos, every blasted newspaper and TV man in the country's trying to break into this camp, and we've got to take a little kid out there to do our job for us? I don't like it."

Sergeant Warner looked as if he wanted to say something, but he satisfied himself with a stern glare in Johnny's direction.

Gene said, "We've got nothing to lose. All our efforts of the past three days have amounted to zero results. Maybe the sight of a youngster will stir them."

One of the civilians shook his head. A colonel banged his fist on the table and said, "By god, a couple rounds of artillery will stir them! Put a few shots close to 'em—make 'em know we mean business!"

"And run the risk of having them destroy everything in sight?" asked one of the civilians, his voice sharp as the whine of an angry hornet.

"This isn't some idiot movie," the colonel snapped.

"Precisely," said the civilian. "If we anger them,

there's no telling how much damage they could do. Do you have any idea of how much energy they must be able to control in that ship?"

"One little ship? Three people?"

"That one little ship," the scientist answered, "has crossed distances billions of times greater than our biggest rockets. And there might be more than one ship, as well."

"NORAD hasn't picked up any other ships in orbit around Earth," the other colonel said.

"None of our radars have detected *this* ship," the scientist said, pointing in the general direction of the glowing star ship. "The radars just don't get any signal from it at all!"

General Hackett took the cigar from his mouth. "All right, all right. There's no sense firing at them unless we get some clear indication that they're dangerous."

He turned to Gene. "You really think the kid will get them interested enough to talk to us?"

Gene shrugged. "It's worth a try."

"You don't think it will be dangerous?" the general asked. "Bringing him right up close to them like that?"

"If they want to be dangerous," Gene said, "I'll bet they can hurt anyone they want to, anywhere on Earth."

There was a long silence.

Finally General Hackett said, "Okay—let the kid talk to them."

Sergeant Warner insisted that Johnny's parents had to agree to the idea, and Johnny wound up spending most of the morning talking on the radio-phone in the sergeant's

State Police cruiser. Gene talked to them too, and explained what they planned to do.

It took a long time to calm his parents down. His mother cried and said she was so worried. His father tried to sound angry about Johnny's running away. But he really sounded relieved that his son was all right. After hours of talking, they finally agreed to let Johnny face the aliens.

But when Johnny at last handed the phone back to Sergeant Warner, he felt lower than a scorpion.

"I really scared them," he told Gene as they walked back to the tents.

"Guess you did."

"But they wouldn't have let me go if I'd stayed home and asked them. They would've said no."

Gene shrugged.

Then Johnny noticed that his shadow had shrunk to practically nothing. He turned and squinted up at the sky. The sun was almost at zenith. It was almost high noon.

"Less than two minutes to noon," Gene said, looking at his wristwatch. "Let's get moving. I want to be out there where they can see you when they appear."

They turned and started walking out toward the aliens' ship. Past the trucks and jeeps and vans that were parked in neat rows. Past the tanks, huge and heavy, with the snouts of their long cannon pointed straight at the ship. Past the ranks of soldiers who were standing in neat files, guns cleaned and ready for action.

General Hackett and other people from the morning conference were sitting in an open-topped car. A corporal was at the wheel, staring straight at the ship.

Johnny and Gene walked out alone, past everyone and everything, out into the wide cleared space at the center of the camp.

With every step he took, Johnny felt more alone. It was as if he were an astronaut out on EVA—floating away from his ship, out of contact, no way to get back. Even though it was hot, bright daylight, he could *feel* the stars looking down at him—one tiny, lonely, scared boy facing the unknown.

Gene grinned at him as they neared the ship. "I've done this four times now, and it gets spookier every time. My knees are shaking."

Johnny admitted, "Me too."

And then they were there! The three strangers, the aliens, standing about ten yards in front of Johnny and Gene.

It *was* spooky.

The aliens simply stood there, looking relaxed and pleasant. But they seemed to be looking right *through* Johnny and Gene. As if they weren't there at all.

Johnny studied the three of them very carefully. They looked completely human. Tall and handsome as movie stars, with broad shoulders and strong, square-jawed faces. The three of them looked enough alike to be brothers. They wore simple, silvery coveralls that shimmered in the sunlight.

They looked at each other as if they were going to speak. But they said nothing. The only sound Johnny could hear was that highpitched kind of whistling noise that he had heard on tape the night before. Even the wind seemed to have died down, this close to the alien ship.

Johnny glanced up at Gene, and out of the corner of his eye, the three aliens seemed to shimmer and waver, as if he were seeing them through a wavy heat haze.

A chill raced along Johnny's spine.

When he looked straight at the aliens, they seemed real and solid, just like ordinary humans except for their glittery uniforms.

But when he turned his head and saw them only out of the corner of his eye, the aliens shimmered and sizzled. Suddenly Johnny remembered a day in school when they showed movies. His seat had been up close to the screen, and off to one side. He couldn't make out what the picture on the screen was, but he could watch the light shimmering and glittering on the screen.

They're not real!

Johnny suddenly understood that what they were all seeing was a picture, an image of some sort. Not real people at all.

And that, his mind was racing, *means that the aliens really don't look like us at all!*

7

"This is one of our children," Gene was saying to the aliens. "He is not fully grown, as you can see. He has a disease that will . . ."

Johnny stopped listening to Gene. He stared at the aliens. They seemed so real when you looked straight at them. Turning his head toward Gene once more, he again saw the aliens sparkled and shimmered. Like a movie picture.

Without thinking about it any further, Johnny suddenly sprang toward the aliens. Two running steps covered the distance, and he threw himself right off his feet at the three glittering strangers.

He sailed straight *through* them, and landed sprawled on his hands and knees on the other side of them.

"Johnny!"

Turning to sit on the dusty ground, Johnny saw that the aliens—or really, the images of them—were still standing there as if nothing had happened. Gene's face was shocked, mouth open, eyes wide.

Then the images of the aliens winked out. They just disappeared.

Johnny got to his feet.

"What did you do?" Gene asked, hurrying over to grab Johnny by the arm as he got to his feet.

"They're not real!" Johnny shouted with excitement. "They're just pictures . . . they don't really look like us. They're still inside the ship!"

"Wait, slow down," Gene said. "The aliens we've been seeing are images? Holograms, maybe. Yeah, that could explain . . ."

Looking past Gene's shoulder, Johnny could see a dozen soldiers hustling toward them. General Hackett was standing in his car and waving his arms madly.

Everything was happening so fast! But there was one thing that Johnny was sure of. The aliens—the *real* aliens, not the pretty pictures they were showing the Earthmen— the real aliens were still inside of their ship. They had never come out.

Then another thought struck Johnny. What if the ship itself was a picture, too? How could he *ever* talk to the starvisitors, get them to listen to him, help him?

Johnny had to know. Once General Hackett's soldiers got to him, he would never get another chance to speak with the aliens.

With a grit of his teeth, Johnny pulled his arm away from Gene, spun around and raced toward the alien star ship.

"Hey!" Gene yelled. "Johnny! No!"

The globe of the ship gleamed warmly in the sun. It almost seemed to pulsate, to throb like a living, beating heart. A heart made of gold, not flesh and muscle.

Johnny ran straight to the ship and, with his arms stretched out in front of him, he jumped at it. His eyes squeezed shut at the moment before he would hit the ship's shining hull.

Everything went black.

Johnny felt nothing. His feet left the ground, but there was no shock of hitting solid metal, no sense of jumping or falling or even floating. Nothing at all.

He tried to open his eyes, and found that he couldn't. He couldn't move his arms or legs. He couldn't even feel his heart beating.

I'm dead!

8

Slowly a golden light filtered into Johnny's awareness. It was like lying out in the desert sun with your eyes closed; the light glowed behind his closed eyelids.

He opened his eyes and found that he was indeed lying down, but not outdoors. Everything around him was golden and shining.

Johnny's head was spinning. He was inside the alien ship, he knew that. But it was unlike any spacecraft he had seen or heard of. He could see no walls, no equipment, no instruments; only a golden glow, like being inside a star—or maybe inside a cloud of shining gold.

Even the thing he was lying on, Johnny couldn't really make out what it was. It felt soft and warm to his touch, but it wasn't a bed or cot. He found that if he pressed his hands down hard enough, they would go *into* the golden glowing material a little way. Almost like pressing your fingers down into sand, except that this stuff was warm and soft.

He sat up. All that he could see was the misty glow, all around him.

"Hey, where are you?" Johnny called out. His voice sounded trembly, even though he was trying hard to stay calm. "I know you're in here someplace!"

Two shining spheres appeared before him. They were so bright that it hurt Johnny's eyes to look straight at them. They were like two tiny suns, about the size of basketballs, hovering in mid-air, shining brilliantly but giving off no heat at all.

"We are here."

It was a sound Johnny could hear. Somewhere in the back of his mind, despite his fears, he was a little disappointed. He had been half-expecting to "hear" a telepathic voice in his mind.

"Where are you?"

"You are looking at us." The voice was flat and unemotional. "We are the two shining globes that you see."

"You?" Johnny squinted at the shining ones. "You're the aliens?"

"This is our ship."

Johnny's heart started beating faster as he realized what was going on. He was inside the ship. And *talking* to the aliens!

"Why wouldn't you talk with the other men?" he asked.

"Why should we? We are not here to speak with them."

"What *are* you here for?"

The voice—Johnny couldn't tell which of the shining ones it came from—hesitated for only a moment. Then it answered, "Our purpose is something you could not understand. You are not mentally equipped to grasp such concepts."

A picture flashed into Johnny's mind of a chimpanzee trying to figure out how a computer works. *Did they plant that in my head?* he wondered.

After a moment, Johnny said, "I came here to ask for your help . . ."

"We are not here to help you," said the voice.

And a second voice added, "Indeed, it would be very dangerous for us to interfere with the environment of your world. Dangerous to you and your kind."

"But you don't understand! I don't want you to change anything, just—"

The shining one on the left seemed to bob up and down a little. "We do understand. We looked into your mind while you were unconscious. You want us to prolong your life span."

"Yes!"

The other one said, "We cannot interfere with the normal life processes of your world. That would change the entire course of your history."

"History?" Johnny felt puzzled. "What do you mean?"

The first sphere drifted a bit closer to Johnny, forcing him to shade his eyes with his hand. "You and your people have assumed that we are visitors from another star. In a sense, we are. But we are also travelers in time. We have come from millions of years in your future."

"Future?" Johnny felt weak. "Millions of years?"

"And apparently we have missed our target time by at least a hundred thousand of your years."

"Missed?" Johnny echoed.

"Yes," said the first shining one. "We stopped here— at this time and place—to get our bearings. We were about to leave when you threw yourself into the ship's defensive screen."

The second shining one added, "Your action was entirely foolish. The screen would have killed you instantly. We never expected any of you to attack us in such an irrational manner."

"I wasn't attacking you," Johnny said. "I just wanted to talk with you."

"So we learned, once we brought you into our ship and revived you. Still, it was a foolish thing to do."

"And now," the second shining sphere said, "your fellow men have begun to attack us. They assume that you have been killed, and they have fired their weapons at us."

"Oh no . . ."

"Have no fear, little one." The first sphere seemed almost amused. "Their primitive shells and rockets fall to the ground without exploding. We are completely safe."

"But they might try an atomic bomb," Johnny said.

"If they do, it will not explode. We are not here to hurt anyone, nor to allow anyone to hurt us."

A new thought struck Johnny. "You said your screen would have killed me. And then you said you brought me inside the ship and revived me. Was . . . was I dead?"

"Your heart had stopped beating," said the first alien. "We also found a few other flaws in your body chemistry, which we corrected. But we took no steps to prolong your life span. You will live some eighty to one hundred years, just as the history of your times has shown us."

Eighty to one hundred years! Johnny was thunderstruck. *The "other flaws in body chemistry" that they fixed—they cured the leukemia!*

Johnny was still staggered by the news, feeling as if he wanted to laugh and cry at the same time, when the first of the shining ones said:

"We must leave now, and hopefully find the proper time and place that we are seeking. We will place you safely among your friends."

"No! Wait! Take me with you! I want to go too!" Johnny surprised himself by shouting it, but he realized as he heard his own words that he really meant it. A trip through thousands of years of time, to who-knows-where!

"That is impossible, little one. Your time and place is here. Your own history shows that quite clearly."

"But you can't just leave me here, after you've shown me so much! How can I be satisfied with just one world and time when *everything's* open to you to travel to! I don't want to be stuck here-and-now. I want to be like you!"

"You will be, little one. You will be. Once we were like you. In time your race will evolve into our type of creature—able to roam through the universe of space and time, able to live directly from the energy of the stars."

"But that'll take millions of years."

"Yes. But your first steps into space have already begun. Before your life ends, you will have visited a few of the stars nearest to your own world. And, in the fullness of time, your race will evolve into ours."

"Maybe so," Johnny said, feeling downcast.

The shining one somehow seemed to smile. "No, little one. There is no element of chance. Remember, we come from your future. *It has already happened.*"

Johnny blinked. "Already happened . . . you—you're really from Earth! Aren't you? You're from the Earth of a million years from now! Is that it?"

"Good-bye grandsire," said the shining ones together.

And Johnny found himself sitting on the desert floor in the hot afternoon sunlight, a few yards in front of General Hackett's command car.

"It's the kid! He's alive!"

Getting slowly to his feet as a hundred soldiers raced toward him, Johnny looked back toward the star ship—the *time* ship.

It winked out. Disappeared. Without a sound or a stirring of the desert dust. One instant it was there, the next it was gone.

9

It was a week later that it really sank home in Johnny's mind.

It had been a wild week. Army officers quizzing him, medical doctors trying to find some trace of the disease, news reporters and TV interviewers asking him a million questions, his mother and father both crying that he was all right and safe and *cured*—a wild week.

Johnny's school friends hung around the house and watched from outside while the Army and news people swarmed in and out. He waved to them, and they waved back, smiling, friendly. They understood. The whole story was splashed all over the papers and TV, even the part about the leukemia. The kids understood why Johnny had been so much of a loner the past few months.

The President telephoned and invited Johnny and his parents to Washington. Dr. Gene Beldone went along too, in a private Air Force twin-engine jet.

As Johnny watched the New Mexico desert give way to the rugged peaks of the Rockies, something that the shining ones had said finally hit home to him:

You will live some eighty to one hundred years, just as the history of your times has shown us.

"How would they know about me from the history of these times?" Johnny whispered to himself as he stared out the thick window of the plane. "That must mean that my name will be famous enough to get into the history books, or tapes, or whatever they'll be using."

Thinking about that for a long time, as the plane crossed the Rockies and flew arrow-straight over the green farmlands of the midwest, Johnny remembered the other thing that the shining ones had told him:

Before your life ends, you will have visited a few of the stars nearest to your own world.

"When they said *you*," Johnny whispered again, "I thought they meant us, the human race. But—maybe they really meant *me!* Me! I'm going to be an interstellar astronaut!"

For the first time, Johnny realized that the excitement in his life hadn't ended. It was just beginning.

13. Plot: Practice

The plot of "The Shining Ones" is basically very simple. It consists of a series of barriers that Johnny Donato must get through, and each barrier is more difficult to penetrate than the one that preceded it.

I started, as with so many stories, with a protagonist: a twelve-year-old boy. What was his problem, the conflict that would drive him, the timebomb that would tick until the story's climax?

It's rather unusual and unrealistic for a boy that young to have a mortal enemy who threatens his life. And make no mistake about it, stories in which the protagonist's life is threatened are the strongest stories. So Johnny had to be threatened by an illness that would be fatal. Leukemia fit the requirement; it attacks young people, predominantly, and although it is almost always fatal, it does not incapacitate the victim until very near the end of its course. Therefore, Johnny could have the fatal disease but still get around and do the things he needed to do.

Once the timebomb is started ticking, it's necessary to show the reader some hope of reaching it in time to prevent the explosion. That hope became the alien ship, and Johnny's stubborn belief that the aliens could—and would—cure him.

Now the writing task came to be one of setting up the barriers between Johnny and his one chance of being cured. As the story was being written, I was somewhat surprised to see the barriers rising like concentric ringwalls, each of them centered on the golden glowing ship and the aliens within it.

The first barrier had already been hurdled by Johnny before page one of the story. That was his parents. Johnny had already run away from home when the story opens. It wasn't necessary to show that, mainly because it would add nothing to the story's progress. Besides, it gives the reader the feeling that Johnny's life began before the story started; this helps to convince the reader that Johnny is really alive.

The desert itself is something of a barrier, but one that Johnny crosses rather easily. Then comes the State Police, first in the person of Sergeant Warner, then in a helicopter, and finally as a couple of searching officers. Johnny eludes them all. Next is the Army camp, drawn up in a circle around the aliens' glowing ship. Johnny slips past the guards and gets inside the camp.

To allow Johnny to succeed even further by himself, without help, would have been stretching the reader's credulity too far, I thought. Besides, there comes a point in a story where you need a second character to give depth and variety; you can't have the protagonist talking to himself *all* the time, especially in a story that is going to be more than a few thousand words long.

So Gene Beldone enters the scene. He comes in first as another test for Johnny, another barrier, perhaps. But he quickly turns into a friend and ally. The next barrier is the general, and Gene helps Johnny to get past him.

Notice that by the time we meet the ultimate barrier, the aliens themselves, we have already planted the fact that they are uncommunicative. The aliens are here for their own purposes, not to help a sick human youngster. They should make the reader feel that perhaps Johnny's labors so far have been all in vain.

This business of planting is an important part of good plotting. You can't have important twists in a story suddenly pop up out of nowhere, with no preparation for them beforehand. The reader's got to be surprised, but not startled or puzzled by totally unexpected twists of events.

If the hero is being held at gunpoint by the villain, and distracts his attention by knocking over a milk bottle, the writer should have planted that milk bottle in that place during an earlier scene, or at least earlier in the same scene. You can't have the milk bottle suddenly appear just for the convenience of the hero. The reader will immediately realize that the author is making life too easy for his protagonist.

There's another side to the coin of planting. If you have an ornate dueling pistol sitting on a character's desk, loaded, in an early scene—it had better be fired off sometime later in the story. Otherwise, there's no purpose to it, but the reader will constantly be wondering what it was doing there and when it will appear again. Such a prop takes on the significance of another ticking timebomb, as far as the reader's concerned and you dare not disappoint him. If the gun plays no part in the story, then get rid of it and don't mention it. Don't clutter up a story—especially a short story—with unneeded props and plants. You may think you're fascinating the readers, but all you're doing is teasing them with promises that you can't keep.

In "The Shining Ones," the aliens' lack of communication with the humans was the ultimate barrier. Johnny gets past that by giving everything he has—including his very life—to break through to the aliens. He succeeds in doing so, only to be told that they won't help him.

But, like the prophecies of the three witches in *Macbeth,* the words that the aliens speak actually mean something very different from the meaning that Johnny at first attaches to them. In essence, this play on words becomes something of a barrier, too, and hides the fact of Johnny's success until the dramatically opportune moment.

If the story had ended at this point, it would have seemed rather anticlimactic and dull: Boy has problem, boy works on problem, boy solves problem. Ho-hum. The reader expects something more, especially in a science fiction story. Something out of the ordinary, exciting, over and beyond the bare solution to the original problem.

It was tempting to try to show much more about the aliens. But that was a dangerous step. For one thing, this is Johnny's story, not theirs. For another, they are much more interesting if they're kept somewhat mysterious. And, frankly, the third factor was that Johnny and the aliens worked out this problem pretty much for themselves. I found myself reading the manuscript as it came out of the typewriter, about as surprised as any reader can be.

We learn a little bit about the aliens, enough to startle us and make us eager for more. They are not really aliens, after all; they are our own descendants, from millions of years in the future, evolved as far beyond our present human forms as we have evolved beyond the tree shrews who were our ancestors.

And it turns out that Johnny has not only been cured of his leukemia, but he has deduced that he will become an astronaut and undertake missions to other stars. His life will go on, and he will become a famous historical figure. *This* is the ultimate reward for his courage and determination: not merely survival, but glory.

It may be that all these techniques and "surprises" were obvious to you as you read the story. If so, then the framework of the plot wasn't covered well enough by the action, characterizations, and background. If the reader can see the machinery working behind each page, then the story can hardly be holding his interest. But if he turns over the final page, looks up and blinks with surprise that he's not still "in" the story, and has returned to the real world with something of a jolt—then the writer has done his work very well indeed.

14. The Science Fiction Market

In the decade of the 1980s one of the fondest childhood dreams of science fiction writers began to come true. Like most childhood dreams, however, this one did not come true quite in the way the writers envisaged, back when they were children.

The most cherished dream of most science fiction writers was to break into the mainstream of American literature: to see science fiction respected, admired, and *paid for* just as if it were an integral part of the literary establishment. This was a particularly American dream because it was mainly in the United States that science fiction had been ghettoized into a narrow corner of the literary marketplace.

The dream is coming true. But in an unexpected way. Science fiction is not breaking into the mainstream so much as the mainstream is coming over and engulfing science fiction.

Here's what I mean.

As L. Sprague de Camp pointed out years ago, the literature of the fantastic was the mainstream of world story-

162

telling from the time writing began until a scant three centuries ago. From Homer to Cervantes, literature dealt with fantastic landscapes, superhuman heroes, supernatural villains—the domain that today we call science fiction or fantasy.

Cervantes' *Don Quixote* was the first major literary work that dealt exclusively with the here-and-now. Its setting was contemporary, its hero and supporting characters were very human.

From then on, European literature dealt increasingly with contemporary tales, or with stories out of history. Real people, doing realistic (even though romantic and exciting) deeds.

By the time Hugo Gernsback began publishing the first science fiction magazine, *Amazing Stories,* in 1926, tales that dealt with fantasy or the future were a minor part of European and American adult literature. Certainly there was an occasional Jules Verne or H. G. Wells, but for every one such fantasist there were hundreds of writers like Galsworthy, Dickens, Hardy, and Melville.

Science fiction enthusiasts often claim that most of the great writers of the past two centuries have written some science fiction. True enough; you can find tales that might justifiably be called SF in the works of Poe, Swift, even F. Scott Fitzgerald. But their "straight" stories far outnumber their occasional dabbles into futuristic or fantastic tales.

When I was young, growing up during World War II, science fiction fans dreamed of a future in which there would be at least one magazine as big and colorful and popular as *Life* or *Collier's*—a magazine devoted to science fiction and the future. But we had to satisfy ourselves with the science fiction magazines that actually existed. Although they were wonderful, they were small in size, circulation, and importance. *Astounding* and *Amazing* were almost the only survivors of World War II. By 1950 they were joined by *Galaxy* and *The Magazine of Fantasy and Science Fiction*. But all of them were digest-sized magazines, weak in advertising, and low in payment to the writers who filled their pages. Their audience was minuscule compared to the national readership of *Saturday Evening Post, Reader's Digest*, or even *True*. Small circulation meant that there wasn't much money available to buy stories.

Television destroyed most of the big magazines, but the hard-core SF audience remained loyal (there was nothing on TV to entice them), and the top rank of science fiction magazines remained in publication, even though many of the lesser magazines failed.

Through the 1950s and 1960s the world saw the first Sputnik, a Space Race that culminated with Americans on the Moon, lasers, quasars, superconducting magnets, spy satellites, artificial hearts, nuclear submarines, and Howard Cosell, brought to you live from anywhere in the world, via Telstar.

What did all this do for science fiction? Not very much, at first. *Astounding* changed its name to *Analog*, and continued to lead the field of science fiction magazines. But the SF audience remained small, although it was growing.

When I became the editor of *Analog*, in 1971, the magazine's circulation was about 110,000 copies per month, more than twice the circulation of its nearest competitors. Seven years later, when I resigned from *Analog*, the circulation was virtually the same. And this was the best, most widely circulated magazine in the field at that time. For six of those seven years I, as editor of *Analog,* was honored with the Hugo Award for Best Professional Editor, which is the highest token of the readers' esteem for a magazine.

The audience for science fiction magazines had not expanded very much, but all through the 1960s and 1970s the market for science fiction paperback books was growing, mainly among college students. Most of them did not realize that science fiction magazines existed. Even teachers of science fiction courses mistakenly believed that all the SF magazines had disappeared during World War II or shortly thereafter.

The science fiction paperbacks soon began bringing out anthologies of new short stories, stories that had never been published before. The market for new writers expanded somewhat, but the pay rates were still low, and most of the new writers were discovered and first published in the magazines.

Science fiction paperbacks were ghettoized in the marketplace; the books were put on their own racks or shelves, so that readers who did not normally pick up science fiction books could easily overlook them.

But in a strange way, the mainstream of American literature was beginning to encroach on science fiction.

You would think that with spacecraft whizzing through the solar system, with recombinant DNA scientists tinkering with genes, with microcomputers getting down to the size of your thumbnail, readers would flock to science fiction to see what might be coming next.

None of those things helped science fiction much.

Star Wars is what did it.

George Lucas may not be the Messiah of our history, but he certainly is the prophet (which can also be spelled P–R–O–F–I–T).

To be sure, *Star Wars* did not spring into the world all on its own. Earlier films, such as *Rosemary's Baby, The Exorcist,* and *Jaws,* convinced the decision-makers in the film industry that there was money to be made in big, lavishly produced films that used special effects to shock the audience. Lucas, with *Star Wars,* turned from shock to almost childlike excitement. Audiences all over the world broke every box-office record in existence to see superheroes and supervillains battle it out against a background of the starry universe.

Star Wars proved that there was a vast audience eager to be entertained with science fiction stories. Why did the publishing industry fail to tap this enormous market until the motion picture industry started to make indecently huge profits from it?

The sad fact is that publishers, of both books and magazines, tend to be exceedingly cautious. For decades their strategy for selling science fiction has been based on the concept of Minimal Success. That is, most publishers based their sales plans for science fiction around the belief that any individual SF book (or magazine) will make only a modest profit, at best.

For most publishing houses, only one or two books per season are earmarked for Maximum Success. These are the top-of-the-line books, the books aimed at the best-seller list.

They get the advertising, the promotional campaigns, the big push with the sales force. If those books sell poorly, heads roll.

But publishers have traditionally treated science fiction, and other "category" fiction, like so many loaves of bread. The books are put on the bookstore shelves or paperback racks. The hard-core audience finds them and buys them. The audience is too small to create major profits for the publisher, but if the publisher can keep its costs down, the Minimal Success book or magazine can bring in a tidy profit. The line as a whole makes a profit, even though individual books in the line may sell miserably. No matter; no one gets fired because a Minimal Success book disappears without a trace.

When I was editor of *Analog*, the magazine was published by The Condé Nast Publications, Inc., a major magazine house. Condé Nast publishes *Vogue, Glamour, Mademoiselle, Bride, House and Garden*—hugely successful slick magazines, heavy with advertisements. *Analog* was minuscule by comparison, and the management rejected every effort to increase the magazine's circulation and profitability. Minimal Success. *Analog* was making a modest profit every month, and the management saw no reason to risk money in an attempt to increase that profit, an attempt that they were convinced would be futile.

The problem with the Minimal Success strategy is that once a book or magazine is earmarked by its publisher for Minimal Success, *it cannot do any better than Minimal Success.*

No matter how good the material inside the book or

magazine may be, no matter how many millions of readers would be delighted by that material if they could only get a copy of it, the book or magazine will sell no more copies than the publisher prints. Shoestring operations produce shoestring results.

Then came *Star Wars*. Trivial as that motion picture was in terms of art, it was a phenomenal success at making money. It literally forced film and TV producers to jump onto the science fiction bandwagon—not an unmixed blessing, since most of them haven't the faintest idea of what science fiction is about. It also made the publishers take a new and serious look at science fiction.

One magazine publisher not only looked; he acted. Bob Guccione, publisher of *Penthouse* and other sexually oriented magazines, had been a science fiction enthusiast ever since he had seen the first Sputnik orbit over Greenwich Village in 1957. The success of *Star Wars* finally convinced him that the time was ripe for launching a big new magazine dealing with science, science fiction, and the future.

Guccione created *Omni* magazine and aimed it for Maximum Success, for an audience far beyond the usual limits of the existing science fiction magazines. *Omni*'s inaugural issue was published October 1978. Within a year the magazine was selling close to one million copies per month, with a total readership of three to five million. *Omni* is also rich in advertising. The magazine became profitable before its sixth issue was published, in no small part because of the millions of dollars Guccione spent to publicize it.

Omni is the first magazine to publish science fiction and

reach a large general readership, far beyond the bounds of the old SF ghetto. Is *Omni* unique, or the harbinger of a new era in magazine publishing? Certainly many new magazines dealing with science and the future have appeared on the newsstands since *Omni*'s success: *Discover, Science 81, Next,* and the revitalized *Science Digest.* But none of them publishes any fiction.

The older science fiction magazines, such as *Analog,* are in a state of turmoil and uncertainty. Still small, digest-sized magazines with virtually no advertising to help support them, they depend entirely on their readers for financial support. As inflation drives the costs constantly upward, they must increase their cover prices to remain in publication. Their audience of hard-core science fiction fans remains remarkably loyal. *Analog*'s readership dipped less than ten percent during the 1971–78 period, while the price of the magazine more than doubled, going from 60¢ to $1.25.

In the late 1970s *Isaac Asimov's Science Fiction Magazine* made its first appearance and quickly established itself, gaining a circulation rivaling that of *Analog.* It was the first successful new hard-core SF magazine in nearly thirty years. But beloved older magazines like *Galaxy* and *Amazing* faltered and dropped out of sight.

Galileo was started earlier than *Asimov's* and achieved a measure of success by selling only through mail order. But early in 1980 that magazine went to newsstand distribution and immediately ran into financial problems.

Even redoubtable old *Analog,* long the kingpin of the field, was sold by its publisher shortly after celebrating its fiftieth anniversary in January 1980. Condé Nast sold *Analog* to Davis Publications, the same company that puts out *Asimov's* magazine. While Davis is a much smaller house than Condé Nast, Davis will no doubt pay more attention to *Analog* than Condé Nast did. These digest-sized magazines, with their small but very loyal audiences, offer the best place for a new writer to break into print. Most of the readers yearn to be writers themselves, and the editors of these magazines, unable to compete financially for the more successful writers, actively seek new talent.

As of this writing, *Omni* is the only big-circulation magazine that regularly prints science fiction. While *Omni* reaches for such "name" authors as Robert A. Heinlein, Ray Bradbury, Frank Herbert, and Asimov himself, the magazine has also published lesser-known writers and even a few total newcomers. Hardly any other magazines publish science fiction at all, although some of the men's magazines, such as *Playboy* and *Penthouse,* will do so on occasion.

The book market for science fiction is where the mainstream is exerting its biggest effect—in a strange, unsettling way.

Several book publishers have science fiction "lines": they regularly publish science fiction novels and anthologies that are aimed at that small, loyal, hard-core audience. Paperback publishers such as Del Rey/Ballantine, DAW, and Fawcett have learned that they can make a steady, if unspectacular, profit from publishing science fiction books for this audience. Minimal Success, again.

Other paperback publishers, most notably Berkley and Pocket Books, have science fiction lines that seem to expand and contract from one year to the next. Dell Books, for example, went from publishing two science fiction titles per month to two per year, a few years back. Then they gradually increased the size of their line until they were just about back to two per month. Most recently, Dell announced it would not buy any new science fiction. How long that will last is anybody's guess.

Among the hardcover houses, Doubleday, Holt, Rinehart and Winston, and St. Martin's Press have regular science fiction lines, with a preset plan of publishing a certain number of books each year. Harper and Row, Houghton Mifflin, and a few other hardcover houses regularly publish science fiction, but they prefer to treat each book on an individual basis.

While most publishing houses, hardcover and paperback alike, have no specific science fiction lines, the list of bestseller books almost any week of the year will include a few books that are set in the future and use as-yet-undeveloped technological gadgetry in their stories. By any reasonable definition, these are science fiction or fantasy novels. Yet they are not labeled as such; they are sold as regular "trade" novels to the general reading audience.

Early in 1980, for example, the *New York Times*'s bestseller list contained four hardcover fiction works of fantasy or the future: *The Devil's Alternative,* by Frederick Forsyth; *Jailbird,* by Kurt Vonnegut; *The Dead Zone,* by Stephen King; and *The Third World War,* written by a team of NATO generals, no less. Tom Wolfe's *The Right Stuff* was on the hardcover nonfiction list for months. Among the paperback best sellers that same week were Stephen King's *The Stand;* and *The Eighties: A Look Back,* edited by Tony Hendra, Christopher Cerf, and Peter Elbling.

Within the previous year, various best-seller lists also included Len Deighton's *SS–GB* (set in an England where the Nazis had won World War II); Carl Sagan's *Broca's Brain* (his earlier *Dragons of Eden* won a Pulitzer Prize); Robert Jastrow's *God and the Astronomers;* and many other works of science or science fiction.

Note that none of these books was written by a science fiction author. Mainstream writers are using such science fiction concepts as alternate history, futuristic technology, futuristic societies and settings, and other "tools" that have been invented and honed over many decades by science fiction writers.

The literary establishment is absorbing these techniques and using them. Ten years ago, a novel like Deighton's *SS–GB* would have been relegated to the science fiction shelves, to seek its fortune there under the Minimal Success strategy. Today there are enough copies in print and enough advertising push behind the book to make it a best seller.

Heinlein has never made the hardcover best-seller list. Nor has Bradbury, Asimov, or Frederik Pohl, despite the fact that, over the years, their books have sold millions upon millions of copies and been much more profitable to their publishers than most of the books in the *Times*'s top ten.

Frank Herbert reached best-seller status with his third

"Dune" novel, *Children of Dune*. Obviously the first two Dune novels built up an audience that is far bigger than the hard-core science fiction readership. Even Herbert's non-Dune works have not sold nearly so well.

To capitalize on the public's newfound interest in science fiction and the future, the book publishers are not turning to science fiction writers. They turn to writers who have proven they can "reach" the general reader and hit the best-seller lists. It is these writers who are bringing science fiction to the general public—in the guise of political thrillers, speculative novels, books of horror or the occult.

This presents a painful dilemma for the new writer. Once you are labeled a science fiction writer, it is very difficult to convince a book publisher that you can write for anyone except the hard-core SF audience. You are typecast.

Arthur C. Clarke once wrote a mainstream novel drawn from his wartime experiences in England. It was titled *Glidepath*. It sold miserably, mainly because the booksellers saw Clarke's name on it and placed it on the science fiction shelves. The SF fans didn't buy it because it was not science fiction, and the other readers never saw it, because they did not go to the science fiction shelves.

Clarke did become a best-selling author with the novel *2001: A Space Odyssey*. Movie and television "tie-ins" are a huge advantage to selling books. Never turn down the opportunity to write a tie-in book.

The field of science fiction is an excellent area for a new writer to learn the craft of writing commercial fiction. The hard-core science fiction market, represented by the digest-sized magazines and the regular paperback lines, offers a marketplace that welcomes new talent. As a writer, you can find a home more easily in science fiction than in any other field of commercial fiction.

But if you dream of going on to mainstream fiction, of reaching out for that bigger, higher-paying audience, then you must be very wary of becoming typecast as a science fiction writer.

Richard McKenna, author of *The Sand Pebbles,* moved from science fiction to Best Sellerdom in the 1960s. After spending some twenty years in the U.S. Navy, "Mac" deliberately chose to begin his writing career in science fiction, because it was the fastest way to learn his craft under actual "battle" conditions. He had enormous talent: His first science fiction story, "Casey Agonistes," immediately established him as a writer to be watched.

McKenna quickly moved on to write *The Sand Pebbles* for that vast general audience out there that never reads science fiction. The book was hugely successful and spawned an equally successful motion picture. Only McKenna's untimely death prevented his becoming a major twentieth-century writer.

As a writer, I want to reach as wide an audience as I can, and McKenna's brief career serves as a model for me. If you want to reach a major audience, then use what you learn from writing science fiction stories to go on and write more ambitious works. They can still contain all the ingredients of good science fiction; the modern reading audience is perfectly willing to read science fiction.

Fear not. The science fiction market today is as large as you, the writer, want to make it.

15. Thinking and Doing

There is much more to producing a good short story than merely sitting at a desk and writing. A great deal of thinking and preparation must be done before you write, and some mechanical things such as typing the final manuscript and cover letter remain to be done after you have finished the story. Here are a few thoughts on these matters.

IDEAS

Probably the biggest misconception that new writers burden themselves with is the notion that ideas are rare and difficult to come by. This is especially worrisome among those who want to write science fiction, where the idea content of the stories is so important.

Yet, as any experienced writer knows, ideas are the easiest part of the job. The air is filled with ideas. Most

175

professional writers have more ideas than time or energy to write about them.

Where do story ideas come from?

Look around you. All the people you know are living with conflict, hope, ambition, love, jealousy, fear—the material for a thousand stories is at your fingertips.

By itself, this material does not make good science fiction. But it is the basic stuff of a good *story,* whether the story turns out to be science fiction or soap opera. All stories are about people, and you have people surrounding you constantly. They will literally give you story ideas, if you are merely observant and patient enough.

How do you turn something that happens to you—say, an argument with a friend—into a science fiction story? There are two things to remember.

First, reduce that argument to a pair of emotional conflicts. That is, take the two people concerned and find out what their internal emotional conflicts were. If you probe yourself honestly this is a good opportunity for a bit of self-analysis. Perhaps you were torn by *pride* vs. *loyalty,* while the person you were arguing with had a conflict of *ambition* vs. *honesty.* Fine. This gives you a pair of characters—a protagonist and an antagonist—to form the central backbone of your story.

The second thing is to ask yourself a question that is fundamental to all good science fiction stories: "What if . . . ?" What if these two characters had that kind of conflict in an L–5 space colony? Or, what if the *subject* of the argument had been something much more serious, such as the decision to unleash nuclear warfare?

Most good science fiction stories are built around that intriguing question, "What if ... ?" Many times a writer will begin with that question, then add people and human conflict to the basic situation to flesh out the story line.

Try a challenge. Take this basic "What if ... ?" question and make a story out of it. What if someone invented a lie detector that is absolutely foolproof? The device can detect whenever a person is lying; it can even show when a person's statements are at variance with the known facts of the situation, even though the person believes he is telling the truth.

Take that idea, people it with characters you know personally, pick a protagonist who already has a powerful internal conflict that this new situation will aggravate and accentuate, and make the background—from clothing to politics—consistent with a society that would use such an invention ruthlessly. See what happens.

Now another challenge. Write down three "What if ... ?" situations of your own, then match each of them with a protagonist and his or her internal conflict. Many writers, when starting with an idea for a science fiction situation, ask themselves a different sort of question: "Whom will this hurt?"

If your "What if ... ?" leads you to a scenario in which the Middle East has run out of oil, find the person who will be hurt by this and make that person the focus of your story. If your idea revolves around a new serum that allows people to become virtually immortal, find out who's going to suffer from this (there will be *somebody)* and make that person the focus of your story.

Watch the human conflicts around you. That is vital for any kind of fiction writing.

For science fiction it is also important to stay abreast of what is happening in scientific research and technological development. During the 1970s, for example, the concept of space colonies—built at the L–5 position between the Earth and the Moon out of metals mined from the Moon, and big enough to house thousands of people in perfect comfort—became an important new theme in science fiction. So did the possibilities of the biological research that has led to DNA manipulations, genetic engineering, and cloning.

If you are going to write science fiction you will need to know what science is doing. New ideas are always popping up, and old ones are constantly revised and sometimes discarded.

I may be highly prejudiced, but it seems to me that one of the best sources for information about science and the future is *Omni* magazine. In addition to nonfiction articles written specifically for the average reader, *Omni* also publishes science fiction and pictorials that show artists' visions of the future.

For more details on what is happening in scientific research, the best journals are the American weekly newsletter *Science News* and the British weekly magazine *The New Scientist*. The American monthly magazine *Scientific American* requires some perseverance to read, but it is an invaluable source of detailed information in many areas of science.

Other science-oriented magazines written for the layman include *Discover*, *Science 81*, *Science Digest*, and *Next*.

To go deeper, there are *Sky and Telescope*, together with several other popular astronomy magazines; *Science*, published by the American Association for the Advancement of Science, which leans toward technical articles on biology and chemistry; the British journal *Nature*, which is technically deep but well worth the effort of studying; and many other technical and semitechnical journals published by professional societies such as the American Institute of Aeronautics and Astronautics.

These journals are usually available at most city public libraries. Even if your library does not subscribe to them, the librarian can probably obtain copies for you through interlibrary loan.

One final tip about ideas. If there is a single short-cut to creativity, it is the trick of *juxtaposition*. For example, when Galileo first heard that a Dutch maker of reading spectacles had invented a device that made distant objects appear close-by, the Italian physicist went out and made himself a telescope of his own, even though all he knew was that a combination of lenses was what did the trick. Legend has it he sawed off a length of church organ pipe for the barrel of his instrument.

That took a good deal of ingenuity. But the really creative thing that Galileo did was to turn his telescope to the heavens immediately, instead of seeing how many church steeples he could find with his new toy. By combining a new invention with an old interest in astronomy, Galileo ushered in the modern age of thought.

Storytellers do the same thing. In mathematics you may not be allowed to add apples and oranges, but in fiction it's always good practice to juxtapose two unlikely elements. Ernest Hemingway, in "The Battler," mixed a young runaway with a punchdrunk ex-prizefighter to produce a classic short story. Gordon R. Dickson, in "Computers Don't Argue," took our familiar computerized monthly bills and turned them into a death machine. Norman Spinrad, in "A Thing of Beauty," took a social-climbing Japanese industrialist and a totally collapsed United States to produce a story of dark humor and stinging comment on both American and Japanese societies.

Ideas are all around you. Observe carefully. Look for the underlying emotional conflicts *within* the people you know; those are the raw materials of stories. Study the scientific literature: It's fun and fascinating, and a treasure trove of "What if ... ?" ideas. Juxtapose ideas freely. Mix and match them until you get a pair, or a set, that strikes sparks in your mind. Then write!

Slanting

Wait a minute. Before you write, have you given any thought to who your readers will be? Do you have a specific person in mind, whom you are writing to? Or a specific publisher?

Every magazine has its own special audience, and the editor of a successful magazine knows what that audience wants to read, and continually produces it. Occasionally the editor will try to lead the audience to newer and, one hopes, better things. But if the editor strays too far from the audience's preferences, the audience stops reading the magazine. And the editor starts looking for a new job.

Book publishers, facing the same situation, hire editors to direct the different "lines" they publish. Not every book will be bought by every reader, obviously. Women who read gothics buy very little science fiction. Science fiction readers tend to keep away from romance novels. Mystery fans buy mystery novels, and trying to interest them in nonfiction books about cosmology is usually a waste of effort.

When you decide to write a story for a certain magazine or a certain book publisher, be sure that you are familiar with the style and format of the stories that the editor publishes. As the salesmen say in Meredith Willson's musical comedy *The Music Man,* "You've got to know the territory." To a writer, this means being thoroughly familiar with the audience you are trying to reach.

There is no sense in sending a hard-core science fiction story to *The New Yorker,* just as it's futile to send an enigmatic tale of frustration and despair to *Analog.* There is no sense in sending a forty-thousand-word manuscript to a magazine that never publishes more than five thousand words of fiction per issue. Nor is there any sense in sending a story that attacks hotel chains and tourism to a magazine that depends on hotel chain and airline advertising.

It does not matter how well your story is written. These realities of the marketplace have nothing to do with the quality of the writing. No editor will buy a story that doesn't fit his or her audience, quality notwithstanding. Before you send an editor a manuscript, make certain that you understand what that editor can buy. Read the magazine before you write for it. Read the books that you will be competing against. I have always found that if I don't enjoy reading the magazine, I will not be able to sell a story to that audience, no matter how earnestly I try.

Don't delude yourself into thinking that although the editor has never before published a science fiction story, he will publish your science fiction story because it's so beautifully done. He won't. It's about as likely as an automobile salesman's giving you a car free because he likes your face.

Even within the science fiction market there are shades of difference. Stories that sell to *Analog* may not make it with *Omni*, for example, because of the differences in the two magazines' readership. I make a point of explaining to writers that *Omni*'s readers are mostly new to science fiction and do not understand the background jargon that *Analog*'s readers cut their baby teeth on. If you opened a story with a line such as, "The warship popped out of hyperspace eleven parsecs from Aldaberan IX," most of *Analog*'s readers would feel right at home. Most of *Omni*'s readers would feel totally lost.

Understand the audience. Remember that the editor buys what the editor feels will be right for that audience, no matter what the editor's individual feelings may be. I have rejected many a lovely story, reluctantly, because it was not right for the audience I worked for.

If you are in doubt about an editor's needs or requirements, by all means write a query letter. Editors are glad to send out information about their requirements. It saves them the trouble of reading stories that have no chance of making it in their market.

MANUSCRIPT PREPARATION

Make no mistake about it: the physical appearance of a manuscript is important.

Sure, if you're Alexandr Solzhenitsyn any publisher will be glad to take a manuscript of yours no matter what condition it's in. But if you're a new writer, just getting started, you've got to make it as easy as possible for an editor to read your work. He has to read it before he can buy it, remember.

When you go out on a date, you don't purposely wear clothes that will bother your friend, or deliberately behave in a sloppy manner, do you? The same commonsense rules apply to making your manuscript look neat, clean, and professional.

Look at it from the editor's point of view. He or she reads manuscripts every day. It's what he does for a living. He reads long ones and short ones. Night and day. Weekends, too, very often. His eyes are weakening, his stomach's turning sour, his whole body is atrophying from lack of exercise. Imagine how he feels when he gets a manuscript that's handwritten. Or a Xerox copy that is gray print on grayer paper. Or even a manuscript that's been typed entirely in italic script.

The basic rule of manuscript preparation is: Make the reading as easy as possible. Remember, after the editor reads it, a typesetter must read it with the copy editor's handwritten instructions on it. If the manuscript is sloppy at the outset, the editor will never pass it on to the copy editor and typesetter. It will be more trouble than it's worth.

It would be a wonderful world if the editor could read each manuscript with complete calm detachment, weighing the merits of the story strictly on their own, with no thought to the lousy lunch he just had, or the phone ringing at his elbow, or the approaching deadline date. Alas, such a Utopia doesn't exist. So make your manuscript as easy to read as possible; it's going to run into plenty of competition, and not merely from other manuscripts, either.

In general, it takes very little extra work to make the manuscript attractive and professional-looking. It must be typed, and if you cannot type you should certainly learn how to. If you have a friend who can type well, that's fine. But you should learn for yourself. A good carpenter doesn't go running to a friend for help in driving nails.

Use a black ribbon, and a new one that puts *black* letters on the page. Use white paper. Fancy paper is a waste of money, and harder to read. The typing should be double-spaced, and there should be wide margins on either side and plenty of room at the top and bottom of each page. If you get two hundred to two hundred and fifty words per page, that's fine. Three hundred per page should be an outside limit; beyond that the page begins to get too crowded.

On the first page of the story you should have an approximate word count, the story title, your name and address.

It's also a good idea to put a cover page over the manuscript, and include the word count, title, name, and address on that, as well. Counting words is easy. Just pick ten or twelve lines at random from the story and average the word count in them. Then multiply that average by the total number of lines in the story. It's very approximate, but if the editor has any quibbles he'll get an accurate word count for himself.

Some writers staple their manuscripts together, often with so many staples that it's difficult to open the pages and read the story. A simple paper clip will do, unless the story's so bulky that you need something stronger. In that case, put strong layers of cardboard on the front and back of the manuscript and wrap the whole thing with a few strong rubber bands.

Of course you should include return postage and a self-addressed envelope for mailing, in the unhappy event that your story is rejected. Don't expect editors to mail your manuscript back out of their own funds.

COVER LETTERS

It's perfectly okay to send in your manuscript without a covering letter, as long as the manuscript has all the necessary information on it. Most cover letters go unread anyway.

Some writers feel it's necessary to summarize the story in the letter they send atop the manuscript. That's a dangerous thing to do, because a very busy editor might be tempted to scan the summary and not even read the story itself. And no summary can ever be as deep or strong or good as the story.

On the other hand, I've seen countless cover letters that were much better written than the stories beneath them! Evidently the writer was relaxed, loose, and speaking with his own true voice when he wrote the letter. But he was writing (with a capital W) in the manner of a Writer when he did the story. If these newcomers could use the style and grace they show in their cover letters, and forget whatever rules of writing they apply in their stories, they might well become top-flight professionals. They have the talent, but they muffle their own voices when they begin to write fiction.

INSPIRATION AND PERSPIRATION

Everyone's heard the old saw: "Success is made up of ten percent inspiration and ninety percent perspiration." The simple fact is that it's quite true.

All the studying, thinking, idea-generating, talking, and planning in the world isn't going to get a single word down on paper. In the final analysis, it's those long, lonely hours when there's nothing in the universe except you, a typewriter, and a stack of blank paper, that will determine how successful a writer you will be.

It would be easy to wax poetic at this point and try to fill you with enthusiasm and *esprit de corps* about the wonderful profession of writing. Truth is, it's as much work as digging ditches, and emotionally it's the most demanding profession I know.

A writer is always putting his guts on paper, and allowing editors, critics, and readers to take free kicks at him. Isaac Asimov once pointed out that he could read a review of his latest book that consisted of five thousand words of closely reasoned praise and one tiny sentence of harsh criticism. It's that one sentence that keeps him awake all night. And that's the way it is for all of us.

The best advice I ever heard about writing came, naturally enough, from one of the best writers I know: Robert A. Heinlein. He has worked out Five Rules for Success in Writing, which he talked about in a speech at his alma mater, the United States Naval Academy, in 1973. The five rules are:

First: You must *write*.
Second: You must *finish* what you write.
Third: You must refrain from rewriting except to editorial order.
Fourth: You must place it on the market.
Fifth: You must *keep* it on the market until sold.

I won't try to explain those rules, because I'd have to reprint Heinlein's entire speech to do so. Suffice to say that the speech, titled "Channel Markers," has been published in *Analog* and elsewhere.

Writing is hard work. It is lonely work. The hazards and pains, especially at the beginning, far outweigh the rewards. But . . . but . . .

The United Nations has published a book of photographs by the greatest camera wielders in the world, called *The Faces of Man*.

One of these photographs has always stuck in my mind. It shows an African village, where most of the people have gathered around an old, withered man who is evidently the village storyteller. He is at a high point in the evening's story; his arms are raised over his head, his mouth is agape, his eyes wide. And the whole village is staring at him, equally agape and wide-eyed, breathless to find out what happens next.

That is what storytelling is all about.

There is no older, more honored, more demanding, more frustrating, more rewarding profession in the universe. If the only thing that separates us from the beasts is our intelligence and our ability to speak, then storytelling is the most uniquely human activity there can be.

I waxed poetic after all, didn't I?

Bibliography

Listed below are the stories and books mentioned in the preceding chapters, plus a few other books of value to writers interested in the science fiction short-story market. In cases where the stories were first published in a science fiction magazine, I cite the magazine publication, together with a book in which the story has been anthologized. Most of the books cited below are available from the publisher, according to the 1979–80 *Books in Print*. Those that are not are marked with an asterisk (*) and may be available at a public library, especially if the library features a good science fiction collection.

Asimov, Isaac. *Asimov's Guide to Science*, New York: Basic Books, 1972.

———. "Nightfall," *Astounding Science Fiction*, September 1941; *Science Fiction Hall of Fame*, Vol. I, Robert Silverberg, ed., Garden City, N.Y.: Doubleday, 1970; also in paperback, New York: Avon, 1971.

Bradbury, Ray. "There Will Come Soft Rains," *The Martian Chronicles*, Garden City, N.Y.: Doubleday, 1958; paperback, New York: Bantam, 1974.

Clarke, Arthur C. "The Nine Billion Names of God," *Star Science Fiction Stories,* Frederik C. Pohl, ed., New York: Ballantine, 1953.* Also, *Science Fiction Hall of Fame,* Vol. I (see above).

————. *Profiles of the Future,* New York: Harper & Row, 1962, 1973.

Dickson, Gordon R. "Computers Don't Argue," *Analog,* September 1965; *Science Fiction: Contemporary Mythology,* New York: Harper & Row, 1978.

————. "Whatever Gods There Be," *Amazing Science Fiction,* July 1961; *The Star Road* (story collection), New York: DAW Books, 1974.

Ellison, Harlan. "'Repent, Harlequin!' Said the Ticktockman," *Galaxy,* December 1965; *Nebula Award Stories—One,* Garden City, N.Y.: Doubleday, 1966.* Also, *The Fantasies of Harlan Ellison,* Boston: Gregg Press, 1979.

Godwin, Tom. "The Cold Equations," *Astounding Science Fiction,* August 1954.

Heinlein, Robert A. "The Green Hills of Earth," *The Past Through Tomorrow* (story collection), New York: G. P. Putnam's Sons, 1967.

————. "Requiem," *Astounding Science Fiction,* January 1940; *The Past Through Tomorrow* (see above).

————. "Channel Markers," *Analog,* January 1974; also in *Expanded Universe: The New Worlds of Robert A. Heinlein,* New York: Grosset & Dunlap, 1980.

Hemingway, Ernest. "The Battler," *The Nick Adams Stories,* New York: Charles Scribner's Sons, 1972.

Keyes, Daniel. "Flowers for Algernon," *The Magazine of Fantasy and Science Fiction,* April 1959; *Science Fiction Hall of Fame,* Vol. I (see above). Originally a novelette, "Flowers for Algernon" was expanded into a novel. New York: Harcourt, Brace & Jovanovich, 1966; also in paperback, New York: Bantam, 1970.

Kornbluth, Cyril M. "The Marching Morons," *Galaxy,* April 1951; *Science Fiction Hall of Fame,* Vol. II, Ben Bova, ed., Garden City, N.Y.: Doubleday, 1973; also in paperback, New York: Avon, 1974.

Leiber, Fritz. "The Sixty-Four Square Madhouse," *Worlds of If,* May 1962; *The If Reader of Science Fiction,* Frederik C. Pohl, ed., New York: Ace Books, 1968.*

London, Jack. "To Build a Fire," *Best Short Stories of Jack London,* Garden City, N.Y.: Doubleday, 1953; paperback, New York: Fawcett, 1973.

Martin, George R. R. "The Second Kind of Loneliness," *Analog,* December 1972; *A Song for Lya and Other Stories* (story collection), New York: Avon, 1976.

McIntyre, Vonda N. "Of Mist, and Grass, and Sand," *Analog,* October 1973; *Nebula Award Stories—Nine,* New York: Harper & Row, 1975. "Of Mist, and Grass, and Sand" was expanded and included in *Dream Snake,* a novel, Boston: Houghton Mifflin Co., 1978.

Orwell, George. *Nineteen Eighty-Four,* New York: Harcourt, Brace & Jovanovich, 1949; paperback, New York: New American Library, 1971.

Schumack, Scott W. "Persephone and Hades," *Analog,* September 1973; *The Best of* Analog, Ben Bova, ed., New York: Ace Books, 1978.

Spinrad, Norman. "A Thing of Beauty," *Analog,* January 1973; *The Best of* Analog (see above).

Stevenson, Robert Louis. *Dr. Jekyll and Mr. Hyde,* New York: Dutton (Enriched Classics Series), 1972.

Twain, Mark (Samuel Clemens). "Fenimore Cooper's Literary Offenses," *The Portable Mark Twain,* Bernard De Voto, ed., New York: Viking, 1968.

Wolfe, Gene. "The Blue Mouse," *The Many Worlds of Science Fiction,* Ben Bova, ed., New York: E. P. Dutton, 1971*; *Gene Wolfe's Book of Days,* New York: Doubleday, 1981.

The following books are about writing; they are valuable aids to the writer, at no matter what level of experience:

Burack, A. S., ed. *The Writer's Handbook*, 1980 edition, Boston: The Writer, Inc., 1980.

De Camp, L. Sprague, and Catherine C. De Camp. *Science Fiction Handbook, Revised*, Philadelphia: Owlswick Press, 1975.

Foster-Harris, William. *The Basic Formulas of Fiction*, revised edition, Norman: University of Oklahoma Press, 1967.

Graves, Robert, and Alan Hodge. *The Reader Over Your Shoulder*, second edition, New York: Random House, 1978.

McKenna, Richard. *New Eyes for Old*, Winston-Salem, N.C.: John F. Blair, 1972.

Now for some anthologies of science fiction stories and books about the history and development of science fiction:

Asimov, Isaac, ed. *The Hugo Winners:* Vol. I, New York: Doubleday, 1969; in paperback, New York: Fawcett, 1977. Vol. II, New York: Doubleday, 1971. Vol. III, New York: Doubleday, 1977; paperback, New York: Fawcett, 1979.

Bova, Ben, ed. *Science Fiction Hall of Fame*, Vol. II, New York: Doubleday, 1973; paperback, New York, Avon, 1974.

Gunn, James. *Alternate Worlds*, Englewood Cliffs, N.J.: Prentice-Hall, 1975.

———, ed. *The Road to Science Fiction*, New York: New American Library; Vol. I, 1977; Vol. II, 1979; Vol. III, 1979.

Silverberg, Robert, ed. *Science Fiction Hall of Fame*, Vol. I, Garden City, N.Y.: Doubleday, 1970; paperback, New York: Avon, 1971.

The Science Fiction Writers of America produce a Nebula Award anthology each year. The first seven volumes, no longer in print, were all published by Doubleday.

Nebula Award Stories—Eight, Isaac Asimov, ed., New York: Harper & Row, 1973.

Nebula Award Stories—Nine, Kate Wilhelm, ed., New York: Harper & Row, 1975.

Nebula Award Stories—Ten, Anniversary Issue, James Gunn, ed., New York: Harper & Row, 1975.

Nebula Award Stories—Eleven, Ursula K. LeGuin, ed., New York: Harper & Row, 1977.

Nebula Winners—Twelve, Gordon R. Dickson, ed., New York: Harper & Row, 1978; paperback, New York: Bantam, 1979.

Nebula Winners—Thirteen, Samuel R. Delaney, ed., New York: Harper & Row, 1980.

There are many magazines and newsletters about science fiction published by science fiction fans. The definitive news magazine of science fiction is *Locus,* published by Charles Brown, Locus Publications, Box 3938, San Francisco, California 94119.